BEGINNER**GUITAR**
BARRECHORD**MASTERY**

The Beginner's Guide to Easily Learning & Playing Barre Chords on Guitar

JOSEPH**ALEXANDER**

FUNDAMENTAL**CHANGES**

Beginner Guitar Barre Chord Mastery

The Beginner's Guide to Easily Learning & Playing Barre Chords on Guitar

ISBN: 978-1-78933-397-8

Published by www.fundamental-changes.com

www.fundamental-changes.com

Over 12,000 fans on Facebook: **FundamentalChangesInGuitar**

Instagram: **FundamentalChanges**

For over 350 Free Guitar Lessons with Videos Check Out

www.fundamental-changes.com

Cover Image Copyright: Shutterstock

Contents

About the Author

Joseph Alexander is one of the most prolific writers of modern guitar tuition methods.

He has sold over 1,000,000 books that have educated and inspired a generation of upcoming musicians. His uncomplicated tuition style is based around breaking down the barriers between theory and performance and making music accessible to all.

Educated at London's Guitar Institute and Leeds College of Music, where he earned a degree in Jazz Studies, Joseph has taught thousands of students and written over 50 books on playing the guitar.

He is the managing director of *Fundamental Changes Ltd.*, a publishing company whose sole purpose is to create the highest quality music tuition books and pay excellent royalties to writers and musicians.

Fundamental Changes has published nearly 200 music tuition books and is currently accepting submissions from prospective authors and teachers of all instruments.

Get in touch via **webcontact@fundamental-changes.com** if you'd like to work with us on a project.

Introduction

A barre chord on guitar is simply a movable chord shape; a template you can move up and down the neck to easily play any chord you like without too much thought.

One of the biggest challenges for students wishing to progress is facing their first barre chord. They're often quite happy playing songs with open chords like D Major, G Major and A Minor, then suddenly out of nowhere, the new song they want to learn contains a completely unknown entity: B Minor, F# Major or the dreaded Bb7!

When my students come to tackle these chords in lessons, they will often have tried to play them at home, normally with little success. The same issues/concerns crop up all the time:

"The notes are buzzing."

"My fingers aren't strong enough."

"I can't reach."

"I can't get there quick enough."

"It hurts!"

And even when I show them how these issues can be solved, and how a single chord shape lets you play any chord in any key, there are still more questions to answer…

"But how do I know where to put the barre chord shape to create the right chord?"

"If I can play the same chord with a root note on any of the bottom three strings, which one should I use?"

"Why is it so hard to keep strumming while I change chords?"

These questions and more are the reason I wrote this book. The challenges of playing barre chords are encountered by all players at some point, so I wanted to create something that could be a reference guide for all guitarists.

And if you're ever struggling with these devious melodic devices, I want you to remember that I've had some incredible soloists sit in front of me for a lesson who were totally unable to play convincing rhythm guitar… simply because they'd never gotten to grips with barre chords. Needless to say, their lessons had a shift of focus until they could play barre chords like a boss! Remember, most of playing the guitar is playing great rhythm. If you're stumbling over barre chords, you're not going to get the gig.

By the end of this book, you will be able to play every type of barre chord you'll come across in the music you want to play. We'll cover shapes for the following types of barres:

- Major
- Minor
- Dominant 7 (7)
- Sus2
- Sus4
- Major 7 (Maj7)

- Minor 7 (m7)
- Minor 7 flat 5 (m7b5)
- Major 6
- Minor 6
- Diminished
- Diminished 7
- Augmented
- Augmented 7
- Minor/Major 7

Not only will you learn these chords, you'll be also able to play each chord shape in *three* different positions on the guitar neck, with a root note on the sixth, fifth, and fourth string, so you can move between them quickly and smoothly.

However, (and much more importantly) you'll be able to play them effortlessly, without pain, and at any tempo you need without skipping a beat.

Finally, it's important for you to understand that an essential piece of the barre chord puzzle is *knowing the notes on the neck!* Because even if you know how to play the Major barre chord *shape*, it's pretty useless without knowing *where* to put it on the neck to create the right chord. That means as part of this course, you're also going to memorise the notes on the bottom three strings. Don't worry, it's not as hard as it sounds!

So, if you're ready to dive in, grab your guitar and let's learn all about the basics of barre chords.

Get the Audio

The audio files for this book are available to download for free from **www.fundamental-changes.com.** The link is in the top right-hand corner. Click on the "Guitar" link then simply select this book title from the drop-down menu and follow the instructions to get the audio.

We recommend that you download the files directly to your computer, not to your tablet, and extract them there before adding them to your media library. You can then put them onto your tablet, iPod or burn them to CD. On the download page there are instructions, and we also provide technical support via the contact form.

For over 350 free guitar lessons with videos check out:

www.fundamental-changes.com

Join our free Facebook Community of Cool Musicians

www.facebook.com/groups/fundamentalguitar

Tag us for a share on Instagram: **FundamentalChanges**

Chapter One: The Basics of Barre Chords

In case you were wondering, the term "barre" refers to the technique of "using a rigid finger to bar across the strings". The original spelling *barré* is French, translated from the word "barred".

If it makes you feel better, I always assumed it was a Spanish term, as the Spanish had a lot to do with the evolution of the guitar. However, I've been reliably informed it's French, so there we go!

Barre chords allow guitarists to use a single chord *shape* to play a specific chord type (for example, a major chord or a minor chord) anywhere along the neck. They work because they do not contain any open strings.

To see how a barre chord works in practice, strum all six strings of an open E Major chord on your guitar.

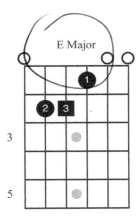

Now slide all the fretted notes one fret higher, so it looks like the chord grid below, and strum all six strings again.

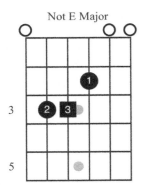

Repeat the process and slide your fingers up another fret, then strum all the strings again.

While you're still holding down *some* of the notes of the original Major chord shape, things start to sound quite weird when you slide them up the neck. That's because you're moving *some* of the notes of the chord shape but not *all* of them. The ringing open strings on the sixth, second, and first strings haven't moved and are therefore "wrong".

If only there was some way to move those open string notes up the neck, along with the fretted notes!

Well, I think you know where I'm going with this… by using your first finger to barre right across the neck, you take those open strings with you as you slide the chord shape up the neck.

We haven't looked at how to fret these chords properly as yet, so don't bother playing the following example – it's just for reference. Take a look at the chord diagrams below and see how adding the barre "preserves" the major chord *shape* as I move from E Major to F Major to G Major to A Major.

Example 1a:

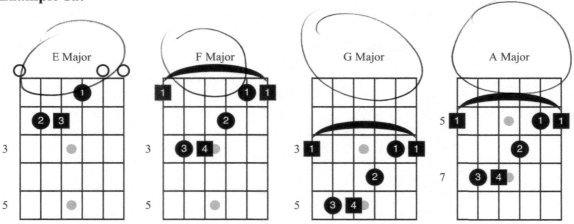

Here's the same process repeated with an E *Minor* chord. Again, you don't need to play this right now, but notice how the minor shape of the open chord is maintained by barring with the first finger. First, I play E Minor, then F Minor, then G Minor and then A Minor… all using the same chord *shape*. Don't play these right now, just look and hear how they work.

Example 1b:

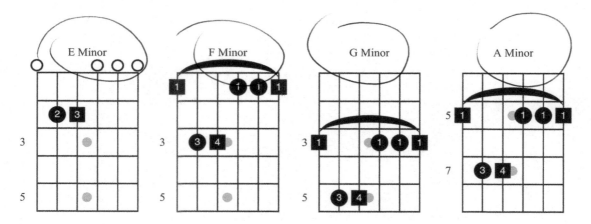

Can you see why guitarists refer to barre chords as "major shapes" or "minor shapes" etc.?

By moving a fixed shape up and down a string we can play literally any chord in any key. That's pretty useful because it means we can play a simple version of any song just by knowing a couple of movable chord shapes.

All we need is to know a barre chord shape for each chord *type* (Major, Minor, 7, Major 7th etc) and where to put it on the neck to make it sound at the correct *pitch* (A, F#, B or D etc).

But to become a really good rhythm guitar player, you should have a few different ways to play each chord type at your disposal. The Major and Minor chords shapes we looked at so far all have their bass note located on the bottom string of the guitar. In this book you're going to learn to play every chord type in *three* different barre forms. One with a root on the sixth string, one with the root on the fifth string, and one on the fourth string.

We're also going to cover the 15 types of chords listed in the introduction. That means you'll g learn 15x3 = 45 barre chord shapes that cover every eventuality – and you'll learn to change between them smoothly while nailing the groove with your strumming hand.

If that sounds intimidating, don't worry! Only around eight of these chord types are common in popular music, so we'll master these first. You'll find the less common chords in a handy appendix at the back of the book.

Now, before we get into the main lessons of this book, let me draw your attention back to the first sentence of this chapter, and the phrase "using a rigid finger to bar across the strings".

At first glance, this definition of playing a barre chord seems to make sense, if you've ever tried playing one. You probably laid you index finger flat across the strings and pressed really hard to make them all sound without buzzing. Then you probably tried to add your other fingers to form a chord, and everything suddenly got a bit uncomfortable.

Sound familiar?

We'll come back to this later, but one of the most important things to know is that your finger will only be rigid *if you're doing it wrong*! Because there's a much easier way to barre the strings, and once you've mastered it, everything else gets a whole load easier.

Now you understand the basics of how barre chords work, let's begin our journey by using the Minor barre chord shape on the sixth string to get our technique right. Once you've got that part sorted, you'll quickly be on your way to barre chord mastery.

Chapter Two: Proper Technique & Minor Barre Chords

Let's begin by taking a look at the proper way to barre across the strings with your first finger. As I mentioned in Chapter One, most students begin by laying their finger *flat* across the strings. This approach has two main disadvantages. The first is that the strings fall into the little finger folds of your knuckles causing them to buzz. The second is that it places your hand in a position where it's almost impossible to comfortably add any other fingers to fret the other notes of the chord.

The secret solution is to place *the side* of your first finger onto the string. Feel it now. There are no knuckle joints to worry about, and it's much harder and bonier than the underside of your finger. Using the side of the finger creates a firm connection between your finger and the strings and has the advantage of placing your hand in a position where any of your fingers can easily reach the other notes of the chord.

To get your hand into the correct position to use the side of your first finger, hold it up with the palm facing you and let your fingers relax and curve naturally.

Next, turn your wrist slightly inward so you can see the outside of your first finger and your thumb points up and across your body.

You can see this position in the figures below.

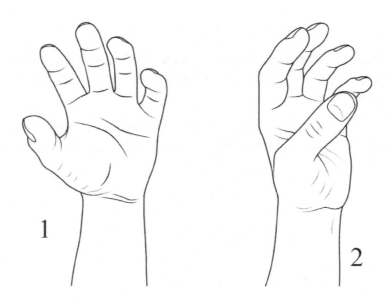

Now let's form our first barre chord. We'll begin by learning the minor barre chord shape with its root on the sixth string.

First, I want you to strum an open E Minor chord so you can see how this open chord becomes a movable shape when we add the barre. However, there's a catch! I want you to use the "wrong" fingers to fret the chord. Instead of using fingers 2 and 3 to fret the notes on the fifth and fourth strings as you would normally, I want you to use fingers 3 and 4 instead.

It'll look like this.

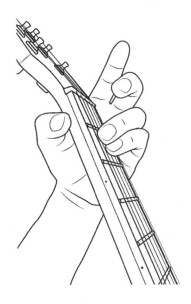
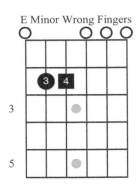

Notice how your first finger is naturally held in a position that's ready to barre across the strings.

Strum all the strings to make sure you're playing the E Minor chord cleanly.

Example 2a:

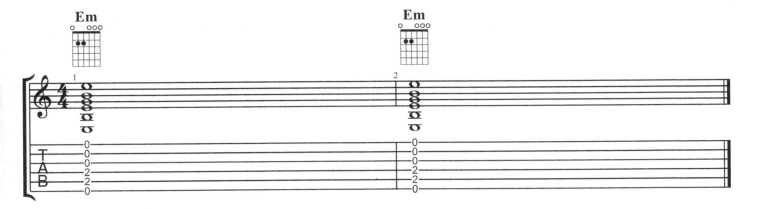

Next, slide the two fingers three frets up the string to the 5th fret. Don't barre yet! Your hand should look like this

Finally, it's time to add the barre on the 3rd fret. Bring your first finger down and lay it across all the strings at the 3rd fret. For most people, it'll naturally want to lie on its side as we discussed above, but if it doesn't, check your elbow. If your elbow is sticking out and there's a clear gap between it and your hip or the side of your body, bring it in until the gap is completely closed. This will help roll your wrist round as described above, and in turn roll your first finger onto its side.

If you've got it all correct, it should look like this:

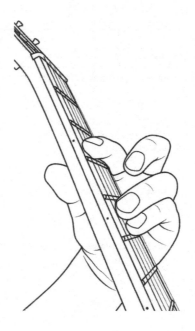

Strum the chord one string at a time to ensure all the strings ring cleanly.

Congratulations! You've now learned the sixth string Minor barre chord shape and you're using it to play the chord G Minor.

Written as a diagram, that barre chord looks like this:

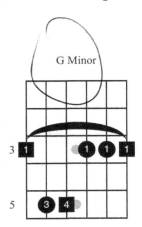

Can you see why guitarists call this "The E Minor Shape Barre chord"? It's an E Minor chord that's been slid up the neck.

Example 2b:

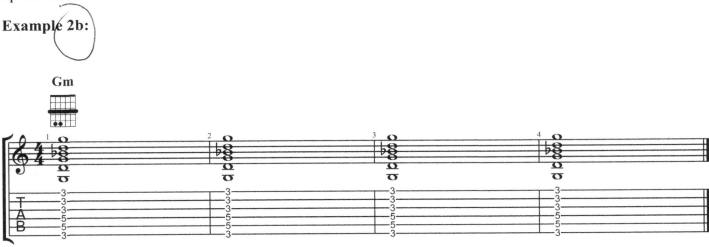

The next step is to program this barre chord into your muscle memory. To do this, we're going to switch between the original open E Minor chord (played with the wrong fingers) and the new G Minor chord.

Set your metronome to 60 beats per minute (bpm). Fret the E Minor chord with your 3rd and 4th fingers and strum it. Hold it for as much of a count of four as you can, before sliding your fingers up to the 5th fret and adding the barre across the 3rd fret with the side of your first finger. Strum it on beat one of the next bar.

Repeat this exercise until you can move smoothly between the two chords. You might not be able to hold down each chord for the full four beats at first. Don't worry about this. Simply strum the chord and begin moving to the next chord as soon as you need to. Just make sure you're there and ready to strum by beat one of the next bar.

Here's that exercise written down for you. Loop it until it becomes comfortable, then gradually increase the tempo on your metronome by 8bpm increments until you reach 100bpm.

Example 2c:

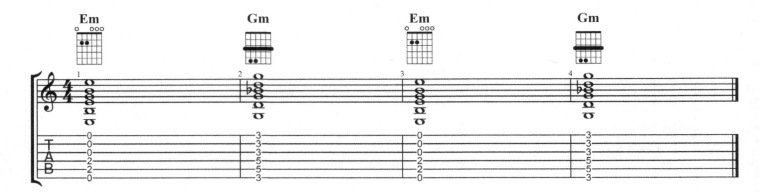

When you're getting the hang of sliding your fingers between positions, I want you to spend some time building your muscle memory in a way that's more similar to how you actually play the guitar.

Play a G Minor barre chord at the 3rd fret, but this time begin by placing the side of your first finger across the strings, then add the other two fingers to form the chord.

Strum all six strings and listen out for any buzzes. Then, simply remove your hand from the neck of the guitar and repeat the process: place your first finger on its side to barre the strings, then add the other fingers to form the chord and strum.

Set your metronome to 60bpm and count along with the click, "1 2 3 4 1 2 3 4" etc. Place and strum the chord on the "1", remove it on the "2", then you'll have beats 3 and 4 to replace the chord ready to strum it on the next "1".

If this is a bit of a challenge at first, try forming the minor shape slightly higher up the neck at the 5th or 6th fret.

Once you're comfortable placing and removing the shape in tempo, try speeding up in 8bpm increments.

When placing and removing the single chord begins to feel natural, try the following exercise.

Play the chord of G Minor (3rd fret), then C Minor (8th fret), then D Minor (10th fret), and finally back to C Minor before looping everything. Play one strum per bar. Set your metronome back down to 60bpm and move between the chords as early as you need to, so that you're ready to strum the next chord on beat 1 of the next four count.

You'll notice that the frets get a bit narrower higher up the neck, so you'll have to adjust your finger positions slightly.

Repeat the exercise until you're comfortable and gradually increase the metronome speed in 8bpm increments.

Example 2d:

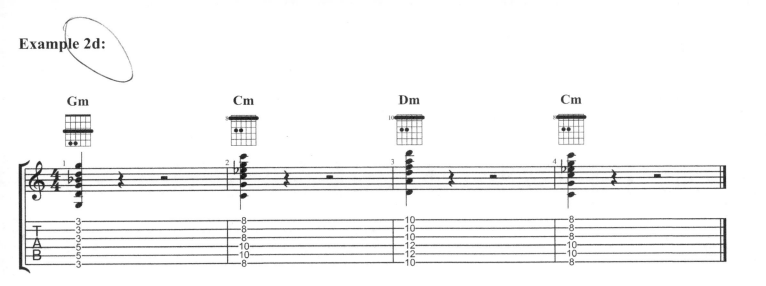

Now, try the same thing but play two strums per bar at 60bpm. It's the same chord sequence but now you'll strum on beats 1 and 3.

Example 2e:

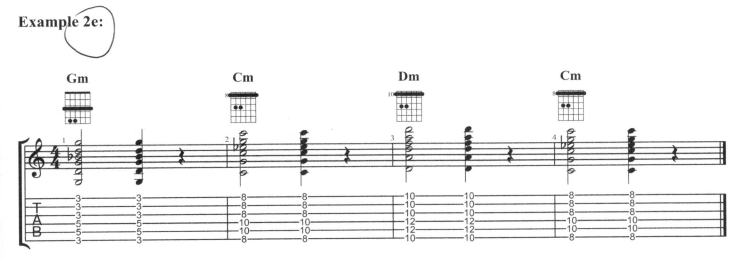

You might want to slow the metronome down to around 50bpm for this next exercise because now you're going to strum on every beat of the bar. This means you'll have to slide quickly between the chords after your final strum on beat 4. Listen to the audio before you play this. Again, when you get confident, gradually increase the tempo.

Example 2f:

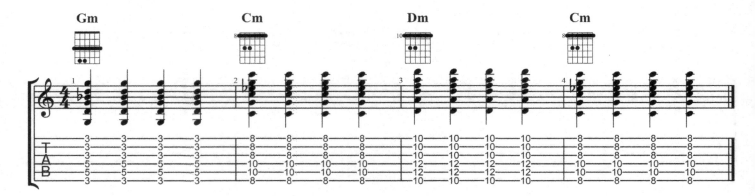

Right now, you might be thinking, "Cool, but what if I want to play a minor chord that's not G Minor, C Minor or D Minor?!"

We'll look at this later, but the short answer is that you can plonk the minor chord shape down anywhere on the guitar neck and the lowest note on the bottom string is what names the chord. For example, if you played the minor barre chord shape at the 5th fret, you'd be playing A Minor.

To play any chord you come across, of course you'll need to learn all the notes on the bottom string, but if you do it gradually it's not too difficult, and we'll tackle this soon. For now, just try to remember the note names of the frets we have used so far. The 3rd fret is G, the 8th is C, and the 10th is D. Don't forget that 0 is E too!

It's great that we can now play any minor chord using a minor barre shape, but it'd be nice to not have to move so far up and down the neck each time. To avoid these big jumps, we can play a minor barre chord shape with a root on the *fifth* string so we can simply move across a string to a new chord, instead of all the way up the neck.

The minor barre chord shape with a root on the fifth string is based around the open chord shape of A Minor.

I've written it here with non-standard fingering, and it might feel a little strange to play it like that, but the idea is to fret the chord in a way that leaves your first finger free to add the barre when we move it up the neck.

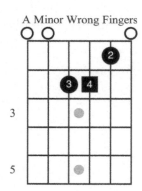

A Minor Wrong Fingers

Strum the A Minor chord using the fingers indicated (top tip: place your second finger down on the 1st fret of the second string first).

Now slide the three fingers up so that your second finger (the one on the second string) is on the 4th fret and the other two are on the 5th fret.

Now add the barre on the 3rd fret using the *side* of your first finger. Don't touch the sixth (bass) string with your finger – you're not going to strum the sixth string because this chord has a fifth string root. (The sixth string is marked with an X on the chord grid, which means don't play this string).

Once again, if you find yourself using the underside of your finger, bring your elbow into your body to rotate your wrist into the proper position.

This chord is C Minor because the root note is the note C on the 3rd fret of the fifth string, and you're holding a *minor* barre chord shape.

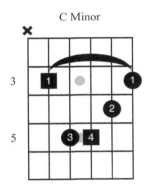

Pick each string individually to hear if they're ringing cleanly. If they're not, look to see if the underside of any of your fingers are accidently touching adjacent strings. If they are, try to play slightly more on the tips of your fingers. It's a common problem for the underside of the second finger to accidentally touch the highest string.

Example 2g:

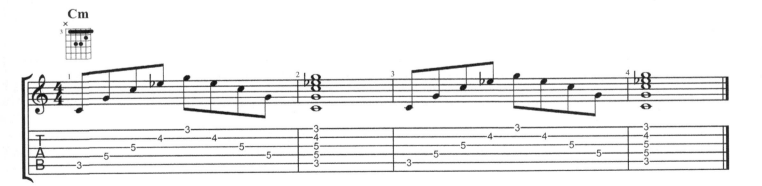

Let's again begin to build some muscle memory. Set your metronome to 60 bpm and strum the C Minor chord on beat 1. Remove it on beat 2, then use beats 3 and 4 to build the chord. Place your finger on its side at the 3rd fret (only on the top five strings) then add the other three fingers. Strum again on beat 1.

Don't worry if you don't play it cleanly at first. Continue playing through the exercise and try to ignore any small mistakes. Repetition is more important than accuracy right now, but if you're really a long way off, slow it down and practice forming the chord without a metronome.

In the following exercise, you're going to move between the C Minor barre chord and the F Minor barre chord that has a root at the 8th fret. Set your metronome to 60bpm and just focus on just hitting the correct chord cleanly on beat 1 of each bar. Don't worry about holding the barre chord for too long, and if you make a mistake, just ignore it and keep looping the exercise.

Example 2h:

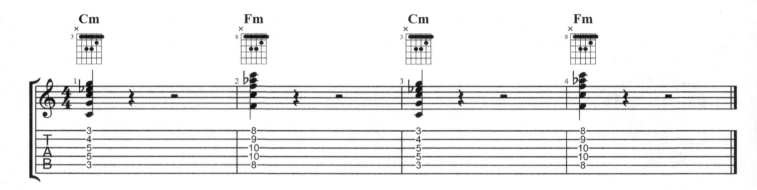

Now you know two barre chord shapes, it's time to shift between them. We'll start by moving between A Minor (played at the 5th fret on the sixth string) and D Minor (played at the 5th fret on the fifth string).

This is the barre chord equivalent of moving between the open chords of E Minor and A Minor.

Begin by placing the side of your first finger across all the strings at the 5th fret and add the two extra fingers at the 7th fret to form the sixth string minor barre chord shape.

Strum the chord and remove your hand from the guitar neck. Don't worry if a few unwanted strings ring out when you move your hand.

Now place the side of your first finger back down, but this time barring across the top five strings at the 5th fret. Add the three extra fingers to form the fifth string minor barre chord shape. Strum the D Minor chord from the fifth string and repeat the process to return to the A Minor chord on the sixth string.

Play the following exercise with the metronome at 60bpm and speed up gradually.

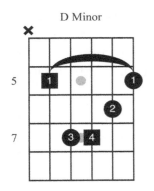

D Minor

Example 2i:

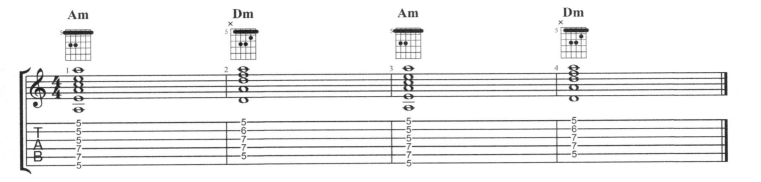

The next example is similar, but you will slide up two frets from D Minor to E Minor on the fifth string, then move across to play B Minor on the sixth string (7th fret), before sliding down to A Minor on the sixth string to repeat the loop.

Remember to remove and replace your hand between each chord and focus on placing your first finger on its side. When your fretting hand gets used to what it's doing, focus on your strumming hand to ensure you're picking the correct number of strings.

Example 2j:

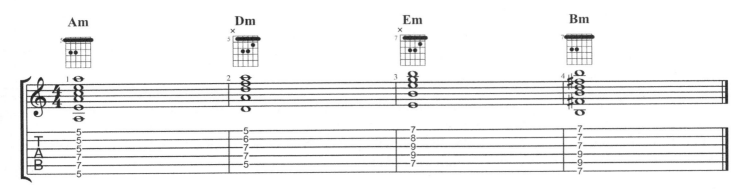

21

Now you're getting used to removing and replacing your hand on the guitar, I want you to repeat Example 2i, but this time try to keep as much of your hand in contact with the strings as possible as you move between A Minor and D Minor. Strum the A Minor chord, then *relax* your hand without removing it from the strings. Slide the whole shape across a string, then add your second finger on the 6th fret to create the D Minor chord. Squeeze the strings slightly and strum from the fifth string.

With practice you should be able to do this very smoothly and keep the strings muted as you do it.

Example 2k:

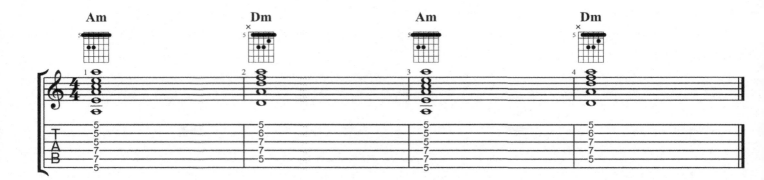

This exercise is similar to Example 2j. The order of the chords is changed slightly to give you some practice at sliding your fingers across the strings and up the frets.

Example 2l:

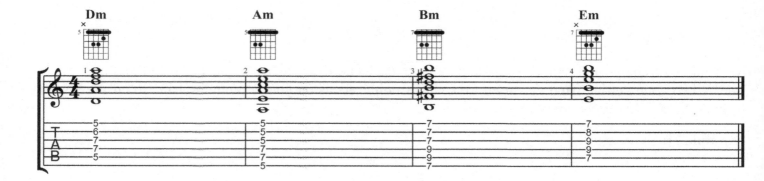

Spend some time coming up with your own chord sequences that focus on moving the minor barre from the sixth to the fifth string.

We've covered the minor barre chord shapes with roots on the sixth and fifth string, so now it's time to learn one with a root on the fourth string. I will say up upfront that this shape isn't used quite as often, as it can be a bit awkward to finger, but it's an important chord to know and is used often in RnB and Soul music to create those high percussive chords that cut through the mix.

The fourth string minor barre chord is based on the open chord of D Minor, shown here.

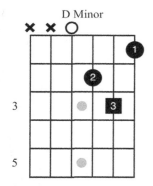

D Minor

Let's move this open chord up the neck and barre it to create a G Minor chord. To play it,

- Place your first finger on the 5th fret of the fourth string

- Then place your third finger on the 7th fret of the third string

- Skip the second string for now and place your second finger on the 6th fret of the first string

- Then return to the second string and place your 4th finger (pinkie) on the 8th fret

The notes in light grey show that while I'm holding the barre across the top four strings, only the lowest note on the fourth string is actually in the chord. This is quite a common approach and occurs a when it's easier to hold a bar than fret a note individually.

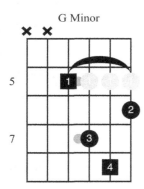

G Minor

If you can't quite reach with your 4th finger, rotate your hand slightly to close the gap between the palm of your hand and the bottom of the guitar neck. Ensure your thumb is roughly in the centre of the back of the neck.

You don't need to press too hard with the barre, as every string has another finger on it. In fact, you don't really have to barre at all, but everyone does as it is much easier.

It should sound like this:

Example 2m:

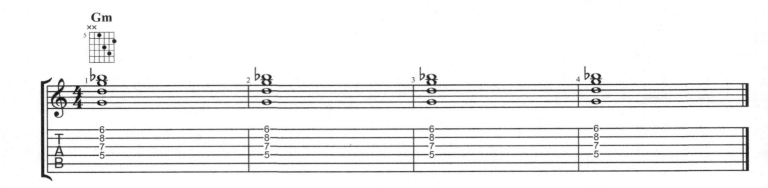

You might find that your little finger is a bit hard to control, so it's worth spending time with this chord building up your muscle memory. Set a slow tempo on your metronome and repeatedly place and remove the barre chord on and off the neck. Hold the chord for two counts and remove it for two counts. It's a great way to spend focused practice time getting your fingers to do what you want, and you can speed up the metronome to gauge your progress.

When you're getting to grips with accurately placing your fingers, move on to the next exercise.

The idea is to strum the fourth string minor shape moving up the neck two frets each time. For this exercise, I recommend completely removing your hand from the guitar neck. While in reality you'd probably slide up the neck if you were playing this in a piece of music, removing your fingers from the neck here will help you build more control.

Example 2n:

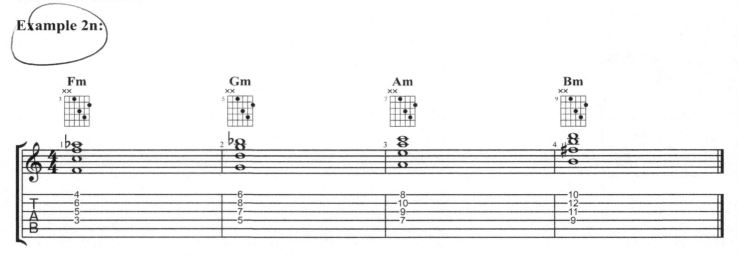

Now let's move between the fourth string shape and the fifth string shape using the chords G Minor and D Minor.

Moving backwards and forwards between these two chords helps to highlight something that many students miss. The fifth string shape has a lot in common with the fourth string shape. As you move it across the strings you'll see that the third and second fingers form the same shape in both chords.

In fact, aside from being on different strings, the only difference between these two shapes is that your little finger needs to move from the third string in the fifth string shape to the first string in the fourth string shape. Take a look at these diagrams and compare the shape of these two notes.

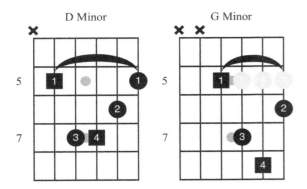

As always, use a metronome and give yourself time to move.

Example 2o

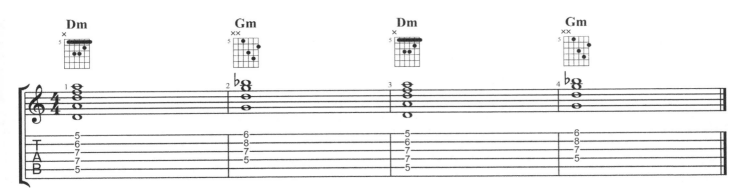

As your confidence with the fourth string minor chord grows, you can start to combine it with other minor chords. The following example uses all three of the minor barre chord shapes to play the sequence D Minor, G Minor, D Minor, A Minor. You might not spot it, but this sequence is similar to the one you learnt in Example 2d where you moved your hand all the way up the neck.

I'm not suggesting you should always play a sequence like this using all three barre chord shapes, as it's definitely a lot of work, but it's great practice for now.

Example 2p:

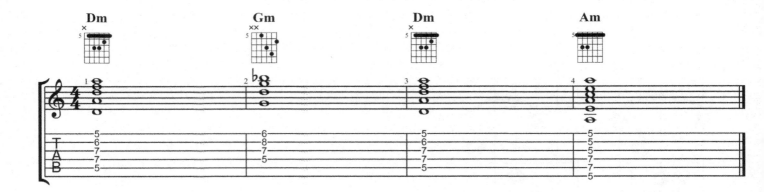

The exercise helps you focus on moving the minor barres between the fourth and fifth string roots while moving your hand up and down the neck.

Begin by playing a G Minor barre on the fourth string at the 5th fret, then slide it up and across to play E Minor at the 7th fret.

Example 2q:

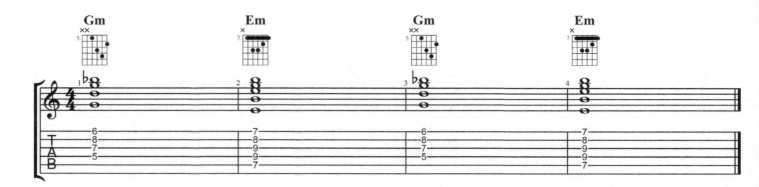

The next exercise is harder. You're going to play three minor barre chord shapes all with the root note of G. You'll begin with the sixth string barre, then the fourth, then the fifth as you work your way up the neck.

Set your metronome *sloooow*. Start with it ticking at 50bpm. Strum the G Minor barre chord on the sixth string and immediately begin to move to the fourth string G Minor. You have the rest of the four count to do this. Aim to place your first finger on the 5th fret then quickly build the rest of the barre chord. Strum again on beat 1 of the next measure.

As soon as you have strummed the fourth string barre, immediately move your hand up the neck to play the fifth string barre. Aim to place your first finger on the 10th fret of the 5th string then form the barre. Again, strum on the next "1".

Next, return back down to the fourth string G Minor and repeat the process before looping the whole exercise.

Please note that this exercise is *difficult*, even for good players. Take your time and aim for accuracy rather than speed. It's all about getting your fingers under control.

One good tip is to try to keep your fingers lightly in contact with the strings at all times and slide them up and down the neck, rather than removing your hands.

Example 2r:

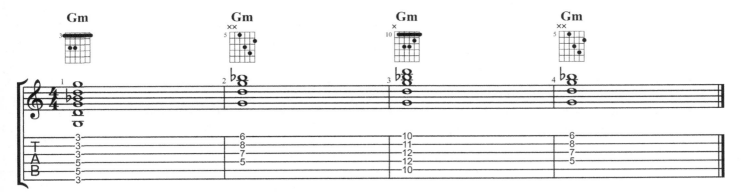

It's important to be able to switch between open chords and barre chords. The following sequence is something you might well come across in your playing. It uses mainly open chords but moves up to F# Minor on the sixth string in bar three. Bonus credit if you play the A Major chord as a barre too!

Example 2s:

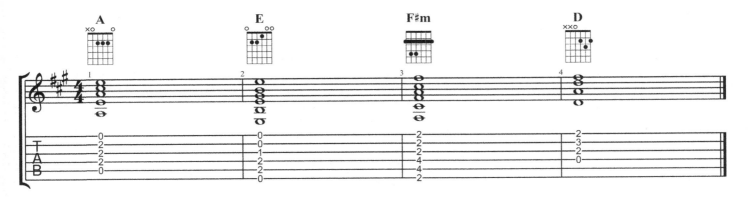

Finally, this sequence uses a B Minor barre on the fifth string. It's a common idea but a bit challenging, because the barre is played so low on the neck. Focus on using the side of your finger and keeping your elbow tucked into your body.

Example 2t:

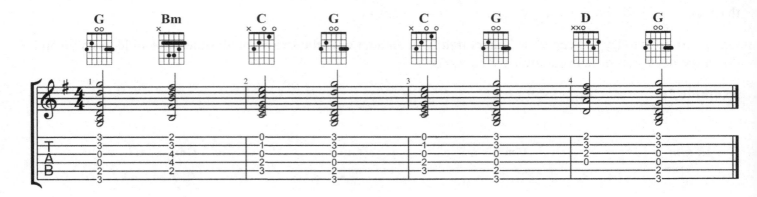

That's quite enough on minor barre chords for now. Let's move on to check out their somewhat more cheerful sounding Major cousins in the next chapter.

Chapter Three: Major Barre Chords

In the previous chapter you learnt that barre chord shapes are created by taking an open chord, sliding it up the neck, then using your first finger to replace the open strings.

The three minor barre chords we learnt were based on the open chords of E Minor, A Minor, and D Minor.

It's probably not going to be much of a surprise to learn that the three *major* barre chords you'll learn in this chapter are based around the open chords of E Major, A Major and D Major.

Let's begin with E Major.

I'll go through the process again that I use to teach students barre chords, but in future you can go through these steps yourself.

Form the open E Major chord shown below but using the "wrong" fingers. Your second finger is on the third string, your third finger is on the fifth string and your little finger is on the fourth string.

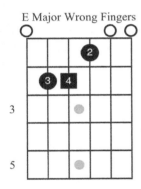

E Major Wrong Fingers

Strum the chord to make sure all the strings sound cleanly without any buzzes.

Slide the chord up the neck so your second finger is on the 6th fret and your other fingers are on the 7th.

Barre with the side of your finger across all the strings at the 5th fret to form the A Major barre chord.

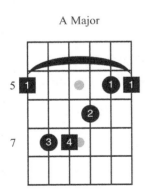

A Major

Pick the chord one string at a time to make sure you're playing it cleanly. Ensure the tips of your fingers are playing the fretted notes.

If you're getting buzzes, ensure your thumb is behind your first finger and bring your elbow into your side.

Example 3a:

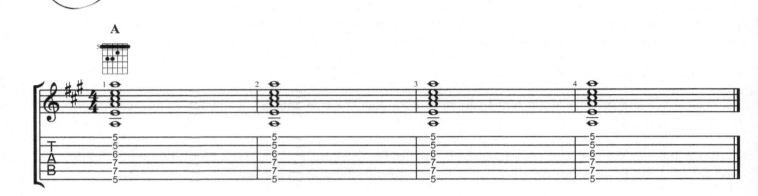

In this exercise you are going to place the chord on the neck, strum it, immediately remove it and use the remaining three beats in the bar to replace it, so you can strum it again on beat 1. Start with the metronome at 60bpm and gradually speed up to 100bpm.

If you find this easy, try strumming the chord on beats 1 and 3.

Example 3b:

Now move the chord up and down the neck. Strum the chord, then relax your fingers before sliding your whole hand up or down the neck while holding the barre chord shape. Try to remain in contact with the strings.

I've written this exercise with two chords per bar, but you can play it at half speed if it's a challenge.

Example 3c:

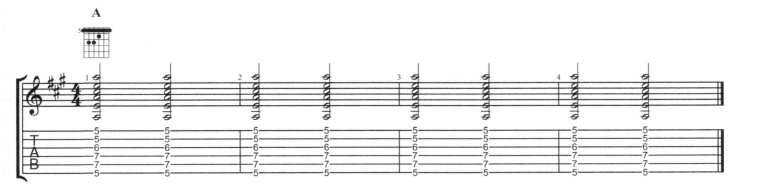

The following example teaches you to move from an open E Major to a barred G Major. Ensure you use the proper fingers for the E Major chord this time as it will give you more of a workout.

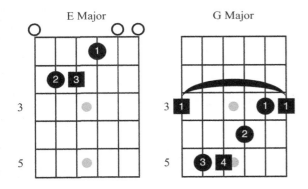

Example 3d:

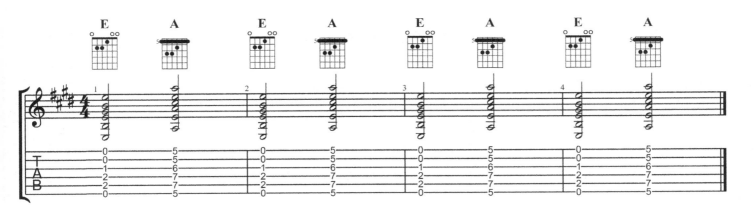

When it comes to the fifth string Major barre chord shape there are a few options as to how you play it.

The "classical" way would be to use three fingers to fret the A Major shape and barre right across the top five strings to access the 5th fret on the top string.

To try this, finger the open A Major chord with the fingering below, then slide it up to the 7th fret and barre across the 5th fret.

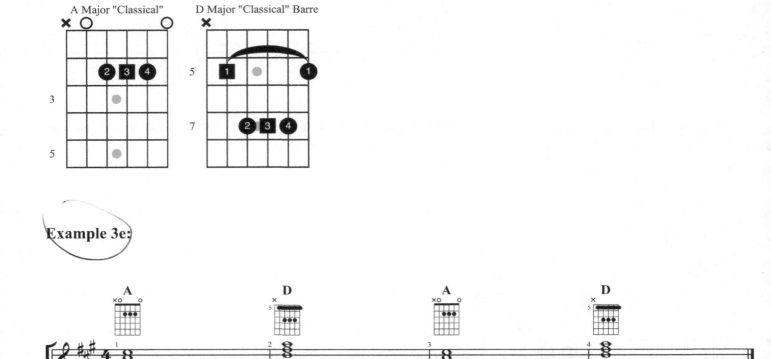

The problem with this is that it's quite difficult to finger and it's also a bit of a challenge to avoid muting the highest string.

Some rock guitarists I know take a slightly different approach and play the whole chord with two fingers and avoid playing the highest string.

All the chords you've learnt until now barre with the first finger, but it's also possible to barre with the third finger, and this is a more common way to play the fifth string major barre chord. Look at the diagram below and pay attention to the way this D Major barre chord is fretted.

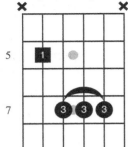

D Major 3rd Finger Barre

If you try to play this as it's written above (by arching your first finger) you may run into difficulties, because what the diagram doesn't show is that your first finger also lays flat across the strings while the third finger barres the 7th fret.

Most people would see the diagram above and try to arch their first finger. The "hack" is to first lay your first finger flat across all the strings, as if you were barring the 5th fret, and also lay your third finger across the 7th fret.

Here's an image of what your hand position should look like:

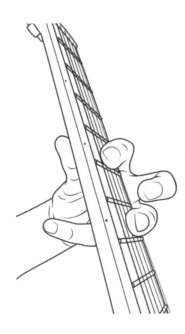

The great advantage of this approach is that it leaves your little finger free to add other tasty notes to the chord. We'll look at some of these shapes later.

The important thing is that you strum only from the fifth to the second string. As you're holding the 7th fret on the first string, you're introducing a note outside the chord and technically it stops being a straight major chord and becomes a Major 6 chord. It's not a bad sound, but it's a bit "country"!

However (because there's never just one way to do anything) there is yet another way to fret a fifth string major barre chord. I don't normally like to give too many options, because it just gets confusing, but this final fingering is also very common, and I noticed myself using it while writing the examples in this chapter.

It's kind of a hybrid fingering that's part power chord and part barre. The idea is to fret a three-finger power chord that you might already know, then lay your little finger down flat to barre the third and second strings.

On paper, it looks like this:

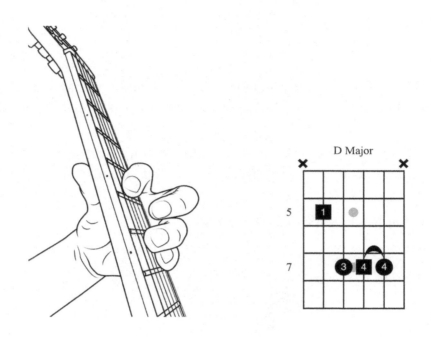

Both of these fretting options are equally valid, and I find myself using them interchangeably.

Try both, and see which is the most comfortable to begin with.

Either way, when you've picked one, stick with it for now and work through the following examples.

First, practice placing and removing the fifth string Major barre chord in the same was you did with A Major in Example 3a.

Example 3f:

Now try moving the chord up and down the neck as shown. Remember to try to keep your fingers lightly brushing the strings as you relax your hand and slide the shape up and down.

Example 3g:

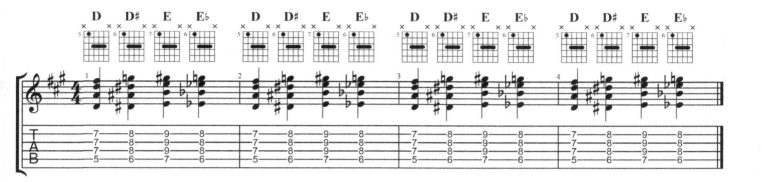

Let's practice moving from a sixth string Major barre to a fifth string Major barre.

Play A Major on the sixth string, then D Major on the fifth. As always, strum the chord on beat 1 and use the following three beats to give yourself time to move to D Major. As you get more confident, try to hold each chord for longer before changing.

Example 3h:

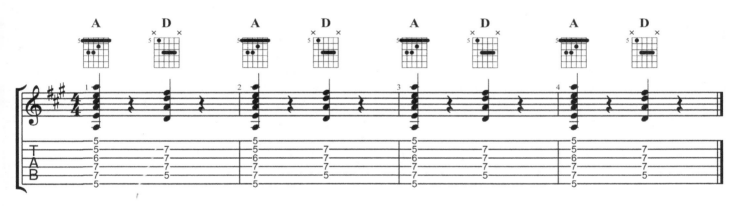

This example moves both across strings and up and down the neck between the chords of G Major, D Major, C Major and back to G Major. The G to D movement teaches you to move both up and across the strings at the same time.

Example 3i:

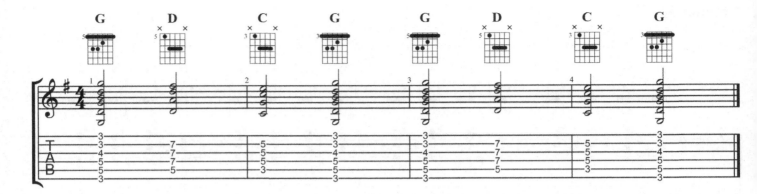

Finally, the next sequence teaches you how to move from an open chord to a Major barre chord on the fifth string.

Example 3j:

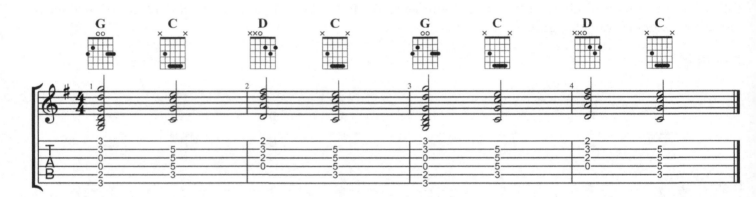

Now spend some time making up your own chord sequences.

Next, it's time to learn the fourth string root *Major* barre shape, which is based around the open D Major chord. Finger an open D Major with fingers 2, 4 and 3. Strum it to make sure it sounds clean, then slide the shape up the neck so that the lowest note is on the 7th fret. Place your first finger across the top four strings to form a light barre and strum it to make sure all the notes are clear.

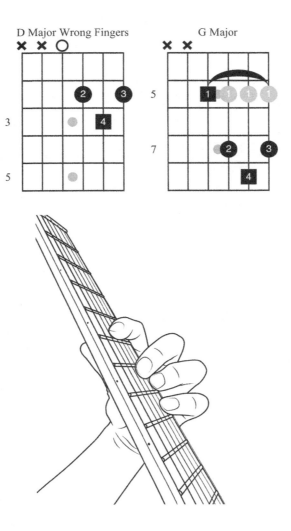

I won't lie to you, while sliding the shape up the neck and adding the barre is a relatively easy way to form the chord, putting your fingers straight down into this position on the neck is difficult. I know that often I, and other guitarists, do tend to avoid this shape and cheat a little bit if we need to play this specific voicing. I'll show you how soon!

However, I wouldn't be doing my job properly if I didn't give you every opportunity to nail this challenging chord shape, so try the following exercises to get your fingers under control.

The easiest way to form the chord at speed it to add the barre last. I tend to put the third finger down on the top string first, then add my second finger on the third string, then the fingers on the second and fourth string kind of go down at the same time. Try it now by simply placing and removing your fingers in the correct positions as shown in the following example.

Example 3k:

When that starts to become easier, you can learn this alternative approach to fingering the chord. Often when playing rhythm guitar, we can get away with playing the root of a chord by itself for a beat and using that time to build the rest of the chord. So this time, try building the chord in reverse by placing the first finger on the fourth string, picking it, and using that beat to add the triangle of other notes on the top strings. This might feel a bit more natural musically.

Example 3l:

Whichever way you choose to play the chord (and eventually you'll be comfortable with both), work through the following examples to solidify the shape in your muscle memory.

First, play the chord, relax your fingers, then slide it up and down the neck.

Example 3m:

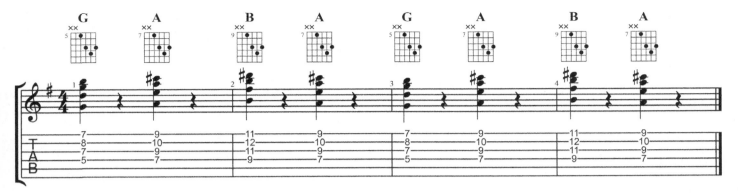

This example teaches you to move between an open D Major and a barred A Major. Don't cheat and use the wrong fingers on the D Major!

Example 3n:

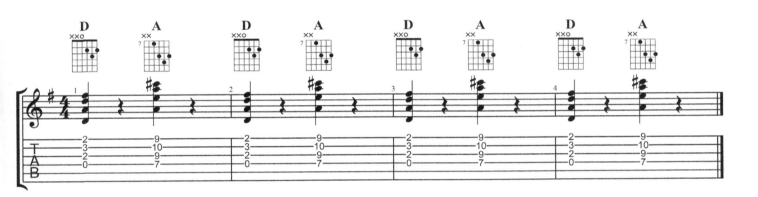

This exercise moves between all three shapes. It's a bit of a finger twister so take it slow. You'll move from G Major to D Major to A Major and back.

Example 3o:

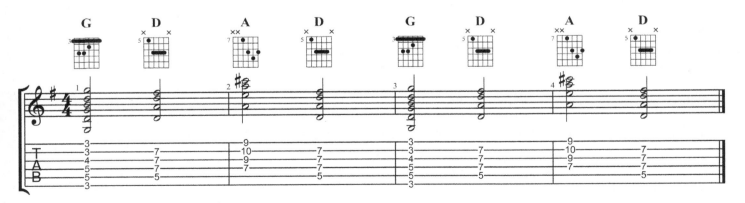

OK, earlier I said there was a cheat that a lot of guitarists use to play this chord… and, in fact, there are two.

First, the simplest way is to just avoid playing the note on the top string and play a three-note chord on the fourth, third and second strings. This is technically not a major chord as it doesn't include the all-important major 3rd, but if you're in a band with another guitarist or keyboard player, it's quite likely someone else will be playing that note.

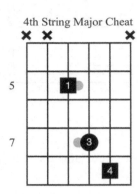

This is really just a power chord and might stand out if it's surrounded by other, richer-sounding chords.

Example 3p:

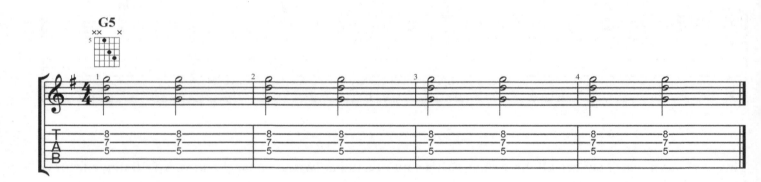

Another way to cheat is to avoid the root note. Again, this works best in a band setting where a bass player, piano or other guitarist is playing the root.

You can play the chord on just the top strings and actually use the same fingering as an open D Major (don't strum the fourth string though!) This voicing omits the root on the fourth string, so it might sound out of place if you're playing solo acoustic guitar.

The other way is to barre across the top three strings and add your second finger on the second string.

Both versions are shown below. The only challenge, especially for beginners, is that you have to *visualise* the root note on the fourth string to make sure you're placing the chord in the right place. In the following diagrams, I've added the root note with a hollow box, so you can see how the chord relates to it, but you should not play it.

Be careful to only play the top three strings and use the side of your finger if you're barring the chord.

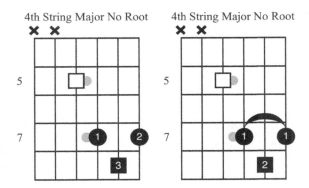

I appreciate I've shown you a lot of options here, which I don't really like to do. Especially for people learning barre chords, it'd be lovely to give you one perfect choice, but unfortunately music just doesn't work like that.

My best advice it to learn the original four-fingered version of the barre chord and master that first. If you really can't manage it, switch to the three fingered version on the fourth, third and second string.

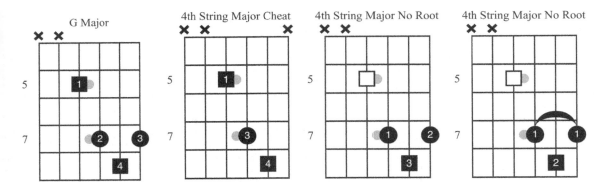

Chapter Four: Learning the Notes on The Neck

As you now understand, we can create a shape from an open chord type, add a barre in place of the open strings, then slide the shape to different locations on the neck to play that chord type at different pitches.

Logically then, the next question is, "Where are all the notes on the neck?"

Unfortunately, the only answer is to learn them.

Some students look down at the neck at this point and see what is essentially a grid of over 100 notes and wonder how they're ever going to memorize them. In fact, when I studied music at university, there were still a few students who didn't know all the notes on the neck.

Imagine being a concert cellist and not knowing all the notes on your instrument… or being a programmer and not knowing all the keys on your keyboard!

Knowing the notes on your guitar is an essential part of being a competent musician and in the next short section you'll learn and memorize the notes on the bottom three strings, so you can use any of the barre chords in this book without hesitation.

The easiest place to start is to learn the notes on the sixth string. We've covered many of these already so hopefully this won't take you too long.

Notice that the open string is the note E, and that repeats at the 12th fret.

There is a tone gap between all the notes except E and F, and B and C.

Notes on the Sixth String

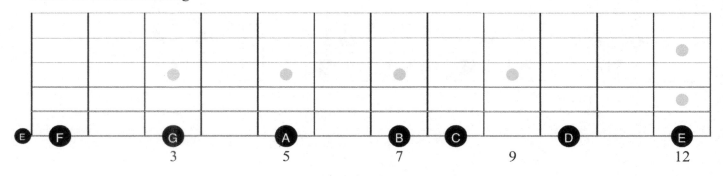

Test yourself now.

Without the book in front of you, play the following sequences of notes on the sixth string.

1) G C A F G

2) D B A C E

3) F A G C B

It's easy to make up short sequences like this to test yourself. Say the notes out loud as you play them to reenforce them in your mind.

The notes *between* the dots above are either sharps (#) or flats (b) and each note can have two different names.

The note between F and G can either be called F# or Gb.

The note between G and A can be called G# or Ab.

The note between C and D can be called C# or Db.

There is no sharp or flat between E and F, and B and C.

As the notes on the top and bottom strings are the same, the following diagram shows all the *enharmonic* names of the notes on the bottom string.

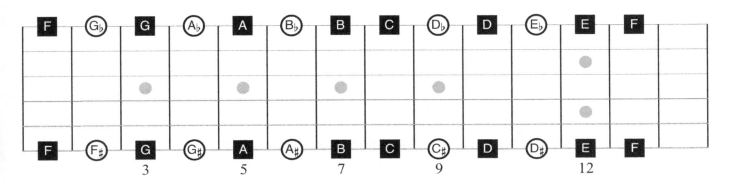

Without the book in front of you, play the following sequences of notes on the sixth string.

1) G# C# A# F# G#

2) Db Bb Ab Eb

3) F# Ab G C# Bb

Once you've learnt the notes on the sixth string you'll know:

If you need to play the chord of Db Major, you play the major barre chord shape at the 9th fret.

If you need to play the chord of G# Minor, you play the minor barre chord shape at the 4th fret.

If you need to play the chord of Bb Major, you play the major barre chord shape at the 6th fret

Next, let's learn the notes on the fifth string.

The following diagram shows the location of each note on the fifth string. Again, sharp or flat notes are located in the gaps between them. E.g. the note D#/Eb is located between the notes D and E.

Notes on the Fifth String

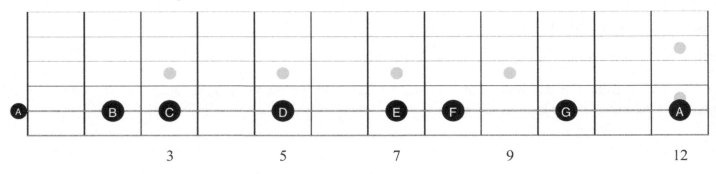

Again, we've covered quite a few of these notes already.

It's useful to remember that the note C is on the 3rd fret (think of strumming an open C Major chord) and that the note E is on the 7th fret (the third dot marker on the neck).

Play and say out loud the following sequences of notes on the fifth string – first with the book open, then with the book closed.

1) G C A F G

2) D B A C E

3) F A G C B

Again, make up short sequences like this to test yourself. Say the notes out loud as you play them to reenforce them in your mind.

Now repeat the exercise with the following sets of notes.

1) G# C# A# F# G#

2) Db Bb Ab Eb

3) F# Ab G C# Bb

If you need to play the chord of Db Major, you play the major barre chord shape at the 4th fret.

If you need to play the chord of G# Minor, you play the minor barre chord shape at the 11th fret.

If you need to play the chord of Bb Major, you play the major barre chord shape at the 1st fret.

44

Now let's combine the fifth and sixth strings.

I want you to play the following sequences using both strings.

Play each sequence twice. Begin by playing the first note on the sixth string, then moving to the *closest* position of the next note, whether that's on the fifth or sixth string.

Then repeat the sequence, but this time begin on the fifth string and move to the closest note in the new position.

For example, in sequence 1, begin by playing the G on the 3rd fret on the sixth string, then move to play the C on the 3rd fret of the fifth string. The second time you play through, begin with the G on the 10th fret of the 5th string, then move to play the C on the 8th fret of the sixth string.

Try each one with the diagrams in front of you first, and then without!

1) G C A F B

2) D B A C E

3) F A G C B

4) A C D G E

5) G# C A F# G#

6) Db Bb A Eb F

7) F# Ab G C# Bb D

Next, you need to learn the notes on the fourth string so you can play any fourth string barre. These always seem a little harder to learn because they're in the middle of the guitar neck. However, there is a nice little trick using *octave* shapes, which we'll learn in a minute, that helps to locate each note quickly.

Here are the notes on the fourth string.

Notice that the open string is the note D and that it repeats on the 12th fret.

The note G is on the 5th fret and the note C is on the 10th fret (two spaces lower than the double dot 12th fret marker).

Notes on the Fourth String

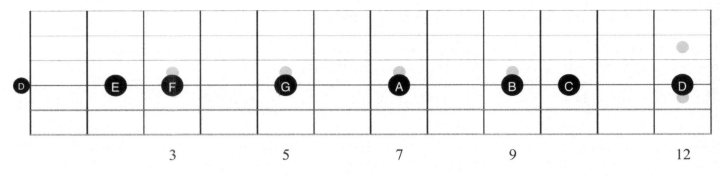

Play through the following sequence of notes on the 4th string with, then without, the diagrams in front of you.

1) E A B F G

2) C B G A F

3) D D G A C B

Now try these using the *enharmonic* notes.

1) G# C A F# G#

2) Db Bb A Eb F

3) F# Ab G C# Bb D

If you struggle with this there's a shortcut you can use to quickly find the location of any note on the fourth string if you know the notes on the sixth string.

Look at the following diagram and see if you can spot the relationships between notes of the same name across both strings.

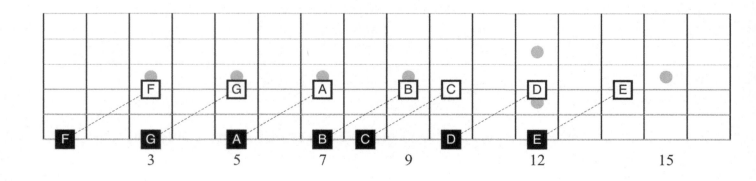

As you can see, every note on the sixth string occurs two frets higher on the fourth string and sounds one *octave* higher.

So, if you're stuck, just imagine this shape and you'll be able to find the notes on the fourth string easily. However, in an ideal world you'll simply memorize the notes on the fourth string and go to them directly.

To round off this chapter, play through each of the following sequences *three* times.

Begin by playing the first note on the sixth string, then by playing the first note on the fifth string, and finally by playing the first note on the fourth string. Move to the closest note each time, whether that is on the same string or an adjacent string.

You may want to have the diagrams above in front of you the first time you play through each sequence, but try to get rid of them as soon as possible.

1) D C A G B F

2) G B F C E A

3) C B G C A E

4) A G D G E

5) Ab C A Gb D

6) Db B Ab Eb F

7) F# Ab G C# Bb D

I hope you found this section useful! In the next chapter we're going to tackle the next most common type of barre chord, the Dominant 7 shape.

Chapter Five: Dominant 7 Barre chords

It'll take a little while to get to learn the locations of the notes on the neck, so I'll continue to give them as we move on to learning these three dominant 7 chord voicings.

Dominant 7 chords (or just "7" for short) are an essential sound in pretty much all music. While this isn't a theory book by any means, you should know that Major and Minor chords contain three notes. For example, C Major contains the notes C, E and G.

Dominant 7 chords are built by adding an extra note to a C Major chord to create a four-note chord. So C7 would contain C, E, G, and Bb.

The added note adds a tense, bluesy, slightly unresolved quality to the sound, and often a dominant 7 chord will want to *resolve* by moving to another chord.

You might be thinking, "Hang on a minute, some of those major and minor chords I just learnt had notes on all six strings!" and while you'd be right, many of those notes are simply doubled up, as you can see in the following diagram.

C Major

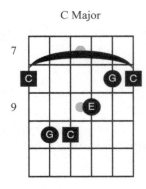

Now look at the diagram of our first C Dominant 7 (C7) barre chord shape on the sixth string. You'll see a lot of similarities with the C Major shape above, but notice how the root note on the fourth string has been replaced with a new note two frets lower.

C7

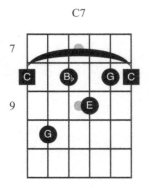

To play this, chord, barre across the neck at the 8th fret, then add your second and third fingers at the same time. Most people find playing C7 a lot easier than playing C Major.

You'll also see that the barre chord is built around the shape of an open E7 chord. If you struggle to play the C7 at first, you can return to our trick of playing an open E7 chord with the wrong fingers, then sliding it up the neck and adding the barre, but by this point you shouldn't really need to.

Strum the C7 chord and make sure everything sounds OK. It's easy to accidentally mute the note on the fourth string with the underside of your third finger, so make sure your fingers are all on their tips.

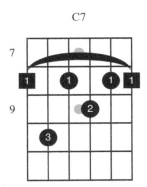

Example 5a:

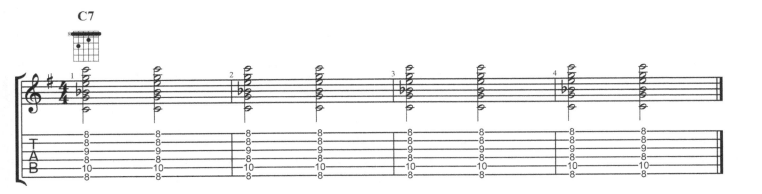

Practice repeatedly placing and removing the chord until your fingers land in the correct places without too much effort. Use a metronome to gauge your progress, as in earlier chapters.

Now it's time to move the dominant 7 shape around the neck. In the following example you'll play G7, C7 then D7, but make up your own sequences too.

Example 5b:

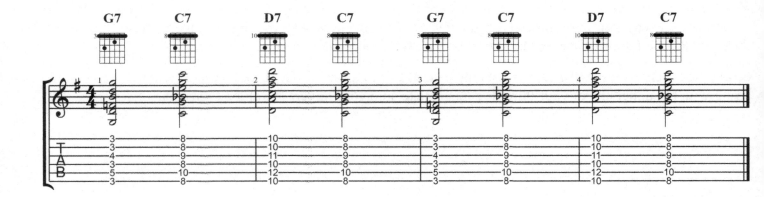

This time practice moving from open chords to barre chords.

Example 5c:

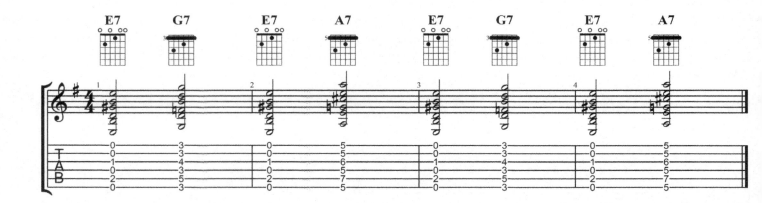

Let's move on to the "7" shape with a root on the fifth string. This chord is based around the open A7 shape. Begin by playing an A7 with your third and fourth fingers, then slide those two notes up to the 7th fret before barring across at the 5th.

You might find it takes some work to get your little finger under control.

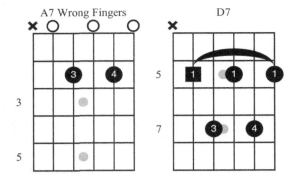

Example 5d:

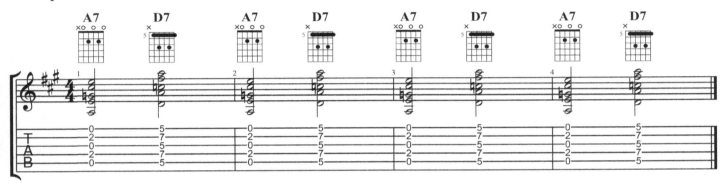

Again, place and remove this chord in time with a slow metronome click until you can form it quickly.

Practice moving this chord shape up and down the fifth string. In this example, you'll play D7, F7 and C7, but you should make up your own sequences to test yourself.

Example 5e:

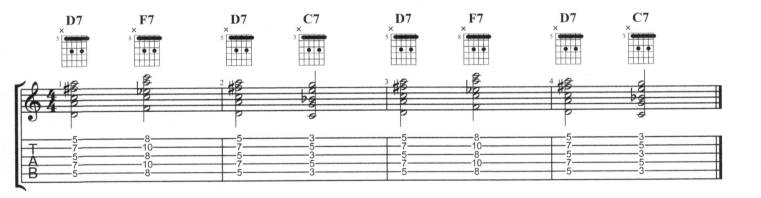

In the next example you'll move between open chords and a dominant 7 barre chord. Use a metronome and make sure you give yourself enough time to change. You don't need to let each chord ring until the end of the bar while you're learning these movements.

Example 5f:

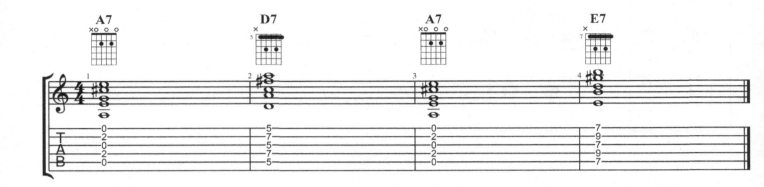

Let's switch between some sixth string and fifth string dominant 7 barres. When moving between A7 and D7, try to keep your fingers in light contact with the strings as you slide your hand across them.

Example 5g:

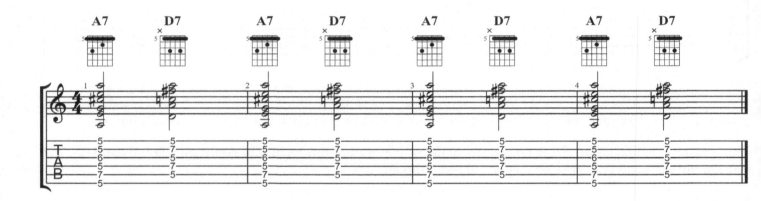

In the next example, you'll make a slightly more awkward movement between A7 and E7 before sliding down to D7.

Example 5h:

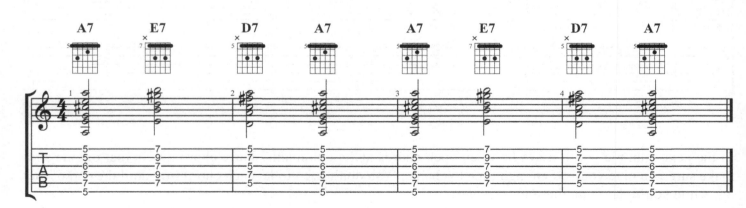

This sequence is quite fun to play. It begins on C7 then moves to E7, F7 and finally G7 before repeating.

Example 5i:

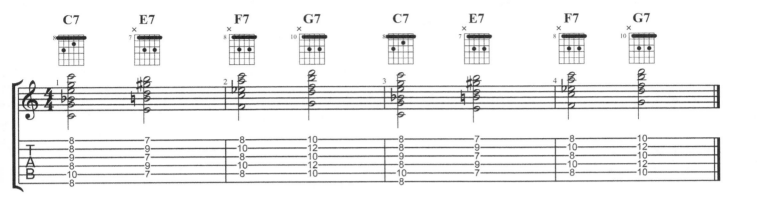

Let's add in some barre chord shapes from earlier. This sequence contains Major, Minor and Dominant chords.

Example 5j:

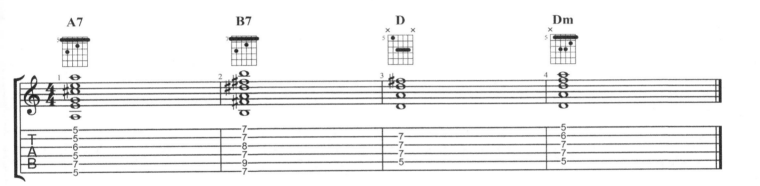

Here's another idea that combines those chord types in a different way.

Example 5k:

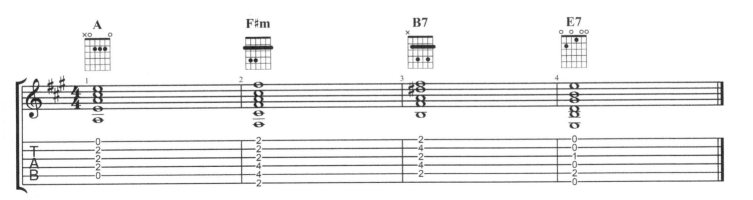

Spend some time making up your own chord sequences before moving on. One useful exercise is to take a song you already know and play it with only barre chords.

Let's move on and learn the barre chord shape on the fourth string. As you might have guessed, it's built around the shape of a D7 open chord. Barre across from the fourth string at the 5th fret and place your fingers in the triangle shape shown below to form a G7 chord.

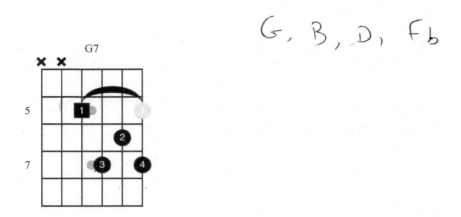

Repeatedly strum and remove the chord in time with a metronome as shown below.

Example 5l:

Now practice moving the shape to different locations on the fourth string.

Example 5m:

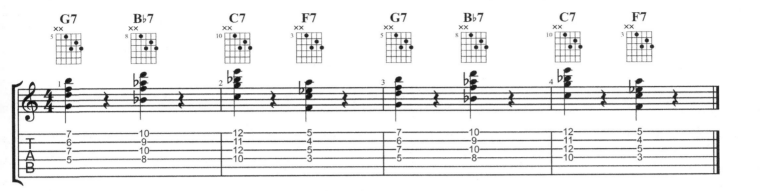

Shift from open chords to fourth string barres

Example 5n:

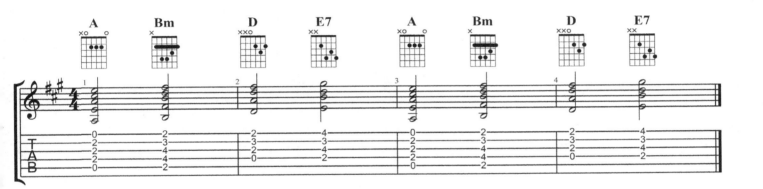

This example combines all three dominant 7 chord shapes as you move from A7 to D7 to G7 and back.

Example 5o:

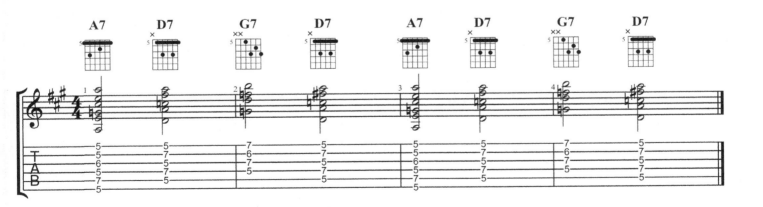

Here's another idea that combines all three shapes in a slightly more challenging different way.

Example 5p:

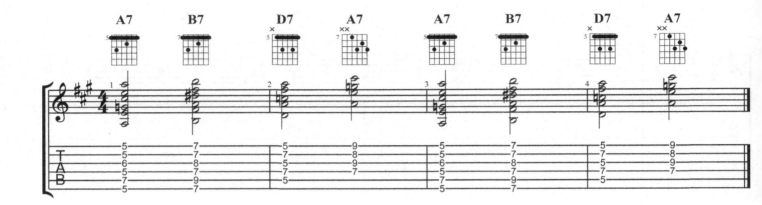

Let's combine dominant 7 shapes with Major and Minor barres.

Example 5q:

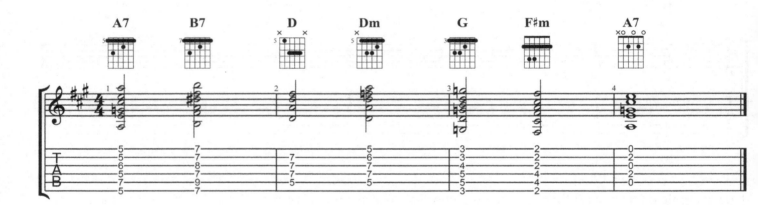

Here's another sequence that combines the three types of barre chords.

Example 5r:

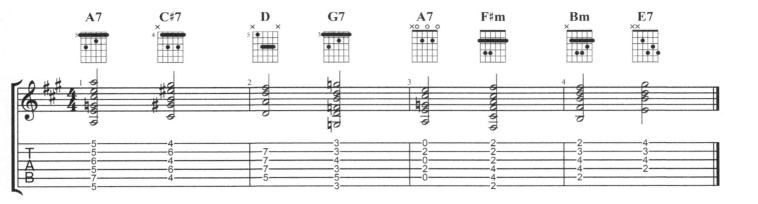

Finally, this chord progression pushes you to move between open chords and all the barre chord types. Take your time and as always build fluency with your metronome.

Example 5s:

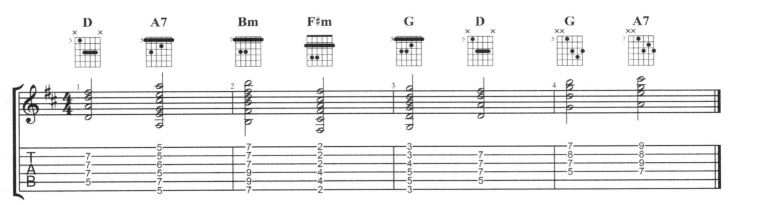

I want to finish up this chapter by giving you some homework. The following six sequences all contain Major, Minor and Dominant barre chords but are written without fret positions.

Work through each chord sequence multiple times, and each time begin in a different place. For example, you could play a C Major barre chord on the 8th fret of the sixth string, the 3rd fret of the fifth string, or the 10th fret of the fourth string.

Each time you change chords, move to the closest possible position available and see how many "routes" through each progression you can find.

When you play barre chords on the fifth string, for example D Major, notice that you could play G Major on the sixth string at the 3rd fret, *or* the fourth string at the 5th fret. Try to make different choices each time and you'll find new paths through the sequence. It's great practice! Remember you can refer to the previous chapter if you forget any of the note locations.

| C | E7 | F | Fm |

| Gm | C7 | Am | D7 |

| A7 | D7 | E7 | D7 |

| Bm | C | F#7 | Bm |

| A | E | F#m | D |

| Dm | A | C7 | F |

Chapter Six: Picking and Strumming Patterns

With these three chord types under your belt, you're set to play most pop and rock songs you'll come across. However, before we enhance your palette with some important but less common barre chord shapes, I want to help you do some work on your accuracy and increase the range of *textures* you can use in your playing.

You might have come across *picking patterns* when you learnt open chords. Well, all of those ideas are totally applicable to barre chords. You might remember that there are two challenges when it comes to playing picking patterns. The first is being able to fret the chord quickly enough to play the pattern smoothly and in time. The second is making sure that every finger is placed perfectly, so there are no muted notes or buzzes.

Both of these challenges return when you start using picking patterns with barre chords, but working through them will make you a much better, more accurate, and cleaner player.

Let's begin with a simple idea. Use your fingers or a pick to play the following picking pattern on a sixth string barred A7 chord. Listen carefully and adjust your fingers if there are any buzzes or muted notes.

Example 6a:

Try this similar pattern with a fifth string D7.

Example 6b:

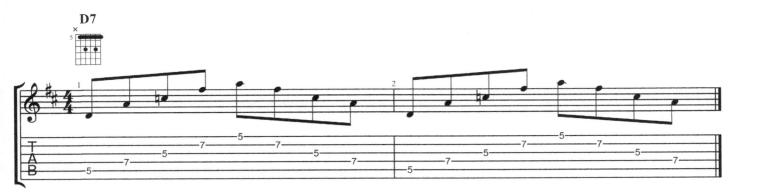

Now play through this pattern using a fourth string A Minor barre.

Example 6c:

The previous sequences used each string in the chord shape so you could easily hear if there were any dud notes in your barres. If you heard any buzzes or notes that didn't sound clean, work through the basic principles of placing your first finger on its side and arching your fretting fingers onto their tips.

When everything is sounding clean, move on and work through the next few ideas.

To build your picking fluency over chord changes, play this example that moves between G Major and C7 on the sixth string. Notice how I've given you a short rest on the final note to give you time to change chord. As you get more fluent, feel free to replace the rest with a pick stroke.

Example 6d:

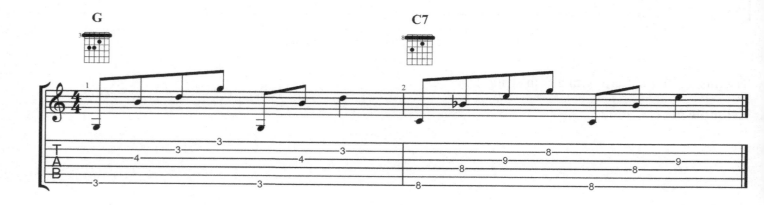

This example takes G Major and C Minor and plays them on different strings. Changing strings is always a little harder than simple moving up and down one string. Again, there's a rest on the final pick of each chord to give you time to change.

Example 6e:

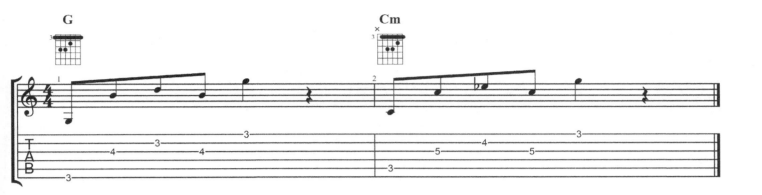

Now try this exercise that moves between the chords of A Major, C# Minor and G7, all played on different strings.

Example 6f:

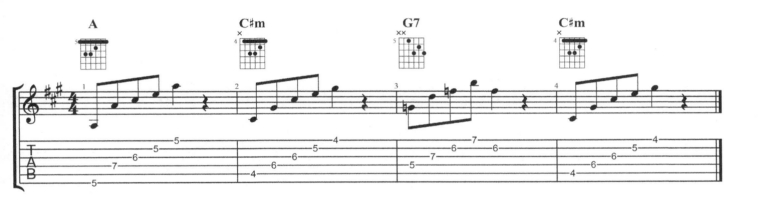

The next example is best played with your fingers so put the pick down for a minute!

The idea is to play the root note of the chord plus three higher strings all at the same time. It's easiest to start with your thumb on the sixth string and your first, second and third fingers placed on the top three strings. Squeeze your fingers in and up (away from the guitar) in a pinching motion to sound the notes together like a piano.

As the chord changes, keep your three fingers on the top three strings, and adjust your thumb to play the root note of each chord on the different strings.

The first example simply moves between B7 (sixth string, 7th fret) and E Minor (fifth string, 7th fret).

Example 6g:

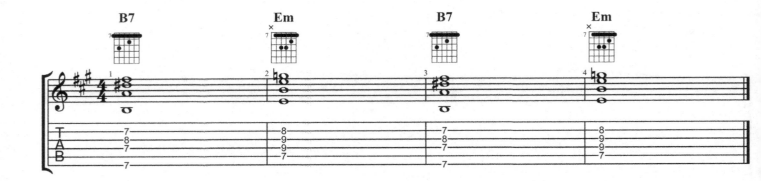

The next idea is similar and moves between D Minor and G Minor on the fifth and fourth strings.

Example 6h:

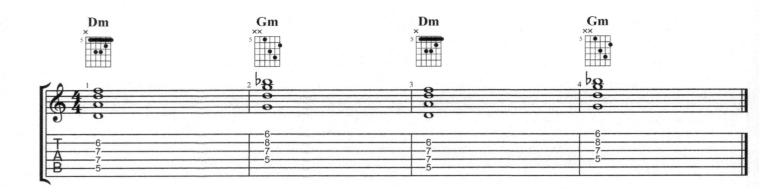

Now move between D Minor, G Minor, A7, then back to D Minor, beginning on the fifth string. Each chord is played with the root on a different string.

Example 6i:

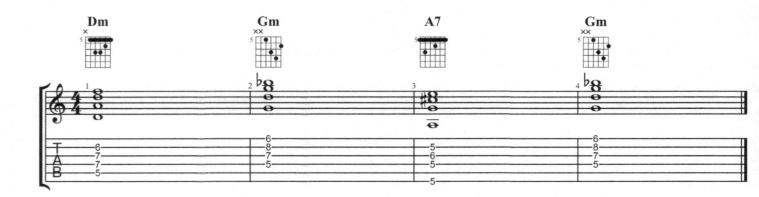

To expand that exercise, begin by playing the pinched four strings together, but only play that on beat 1. For the rest of each bar, alternate between playing the third string and the second and first strings together to fill the time.

Example 6j:

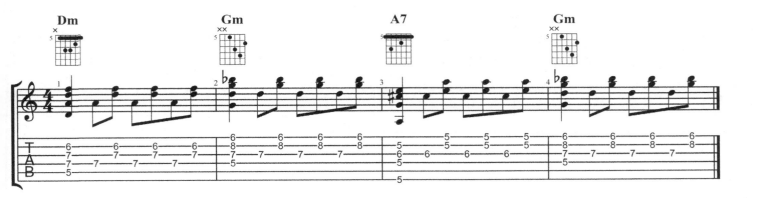

When you play barre chords with roots on the sixth and fifth strings you can move the group of three fingers onto the fourth, third and second strings and basically play the same idea. Try it and see what you can come up with.

I don't want to go down a rabbit hole of picking patterns in this book, I just wanted to give you a few ideas that you can use to check how cleanly you're playing each barre chord. Any picking or strumming patterns you already know will work nicely and begin to add some musicality to your barres.

For a complete guide to these subjects check out my books **The First 100 Picking Patterns for Guitar** and **The First 100 Strumming Patterns for Guitar**.

Before we move on, I want to show you a few strumming patterns that are particularly useful for barre chord ideas. They revolve around the idea of splitting the chord into a bass part and a high part.

The first pattern places a low, isolated bass strum on beats 1 and 3, and a higher isolated strum on the top strings of the guitar on beats 2 and 4.

If you're not sure how to interpret the notation below, listen to the audio track and copy its feel.

Example 6k:

This example adds a *down-up* strum on beats 2 and 4.

Example 6l:

This example places a down strum only on beat 1 of the bar and fills out the time with *down-up* strums on the final three beats of the bar.

Example 6m:

Now try missing out the up strum on beat 3.

Example 6n:

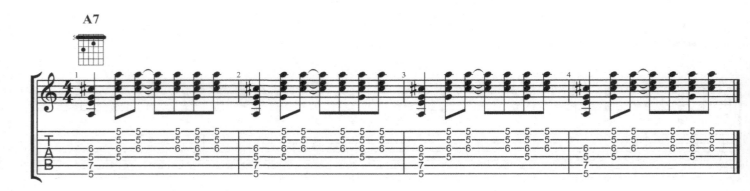

As you can hear, these types of strumming patterns are great for separating out the *voices* (the bass and treble) of the chords and gives other instruments room to breathe.

Listen to the music that you like and look out for how the guitarist separates the voices in their chords.

Spend some time working through the examples in this chapter, then work through the book again adding your favourite strumming and picking patterns to the chord changes we've covered. Start slowly with a metronome – you'll quickly hear where your chord changes need a little extra practice to help you play in time. Return to this chapter later when you have learned some more chords.

Remember, you can take any song you know and play it with barre chords instead of open chords. This is great practice as you have a definite goal to aim for. Try to copy the feel of the track you're trying to play and you'll quickly improve your skills.

Chapter Seven: Suspended Chords

With Major, Minor and Dominant 7 chord shapes under your belt, you're pretty much set to play most pop and rock songs you'll come across, as these are the three most common chord types used. However, the world of barre chords is just opening up to you, so let's continue our exploration of these sounds by learning some other common additions.

Suspended (sus) chords are common in pop and rock and are formed by replacing one of the notes of a Major chord with another. There are two types of suspended chords: sus2 and sus4.

The C Major chord contains the notes C, E and G. The note E is the Major 3rd

In a sus2 chord the note E is replaced by the second note of the scale (D), so a Csus2 chord contains the notes C, **D** and G.

In a sus4 chord the note E is replaced by the fourth note of the scale (F) so a Csus4 chord contains the notes C, **F** and G.

Suspended chords are so called because replacing the very important and stable 3rd of the chord creates an unresolved or "suspended" sound, which naturally wants to resolve somewhere. Normally it resolves back to the same major chord.

For this reason, you will often see chord sequences that contain the movement Csus4 to C Major, or Csus2 to C Major. It's a very common sound and used to create a small amount of tension in the harmony or delay a resolution back to the home key.

This is very easy to hear and play with an open D Major chord.

Below is a chord diagram for D Major, followed by Dsus2 and Dsus4 diagrams. To move between them you simply need to remove or add one finger on the top string.

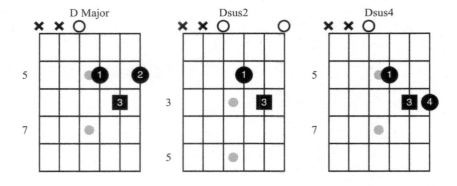

Play through them as follows. Notice how the top note of Dsus2 wants to resolve *upwards* to D Major, and the top note of Dsus4 wants to resolve *downwards* to D Major.

Example 7a:

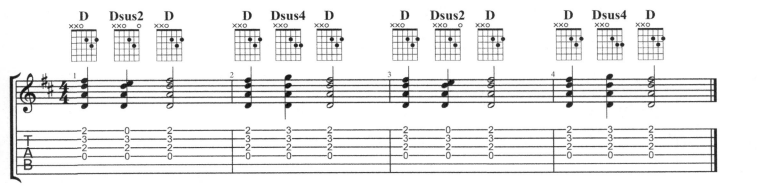

Go and listen to *Crazy Little Thing Called Love* by Queen to hear a whole song that's been written around the movement from D Major to Dsus4.

Because of the nature of the guitar's tuning, it's actually quite difficult to play sus2 and sus4 barre chords with roots on the sixth string and you'll find that most players tend to voice them with roots on the fifth and fourth strings.

We'll come back to the sixth string later, but let's begin by learning the more useful sus2 and sus4 barre chord voicings on the fifth string.

I want you to learn them in conjunction with major barre chord shapes, so you can quickly figure out how to move between them. This is a useful approach because you'll come across this idea in lots of songs.

Begin by playing the three-fingered version of D Major. Place your first finger on the 5th fret of the fifth string and barre across the frets.

Place your third finger on the 7th fret of the fourth string.

Barre the 7th fret on the fourth and third strings with your little finger to complete the D Major chord.

Strum the middle four strings.

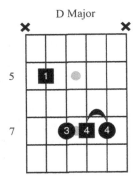

Next, ensure you're barring properly at the fifth fret and roll your fretting fingers onto their tips. This will remove the barre at the 7th fret and allow the 5th fret to sound on the second string.

Again, strum the middle four strings, this time to play a Dsus2 barre chord voicing.

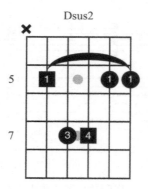

Example 7b:

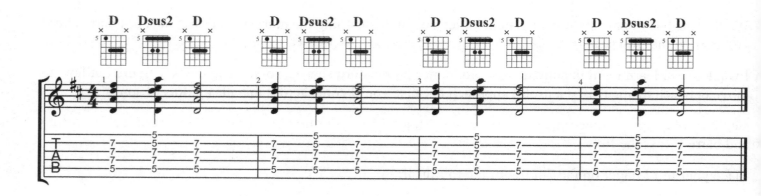

Return to the D Major chord and this time reach out your little finger to play the 8th fret on the second string. You'll need to adjust your third finger to barre both the notes on the 7th fret.

Strum the four middle strings to play a common Dsus4 voicing.

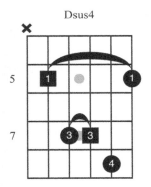

Dsus4

Now practice moving between all three voicings as shown in the following example. It begins on Dsus4.

Example 7c:

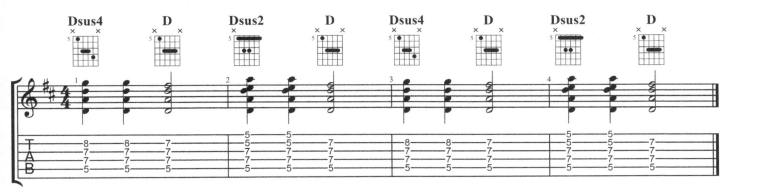

The next example adds a bit of rhythm to the previous sequence and also moves the whole passage up a tone to play Esus4, E Major, Esus2 then E Major again.

Example 7d:

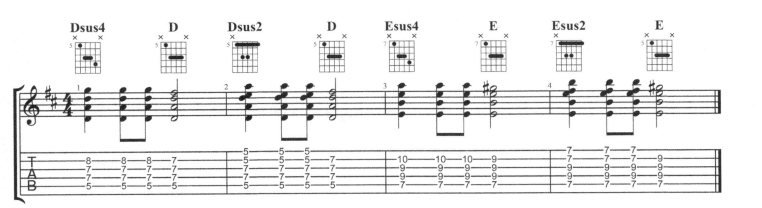

The following diagrams show you the fourth string barre chords of G Major, Gsus4 and Gsus2. Begin by playing the G Major as shown, then flatten your fourth finger to barre across the top two strings to create Gsus4. Remove the finger to create Gsus2

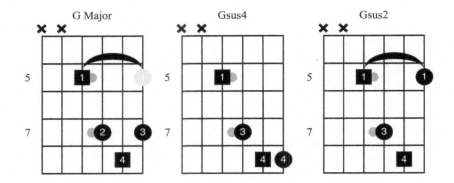

These chords are quite fiddly at first and you'll probably need to spend some time with a metronome to speed them up. Remember that you can always play the rootless voicings to make them easier.

The following ideas combine suspended chords on different strings with other barre shapes.

This example adds a bit of rhythm to the three chords.

Example 7e:

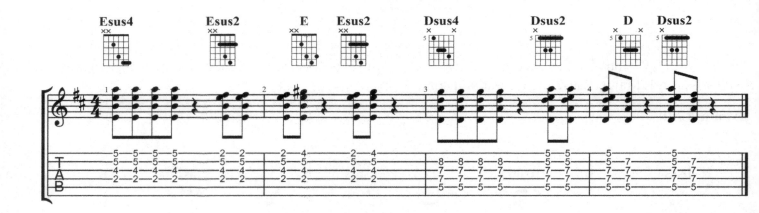

This idea combings a sixth string A Major barre with a Dsus4 to D Major movement.

Example 7f:

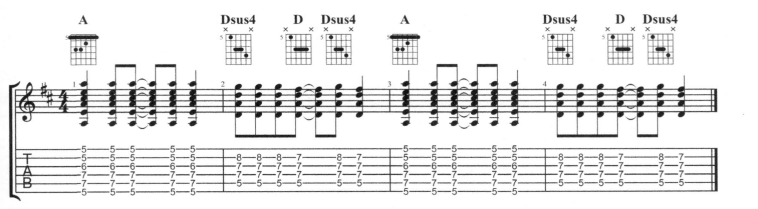

Here's a Dsus2 to D Major idea that resolves to a G Major sixth string barre.

Example 7g:

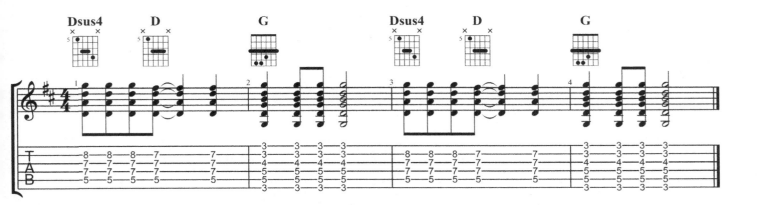

This example combines D and E Major chords on the fourth and fifth strings with a sus4 to major resolution on the fourth string.

Example 7h:

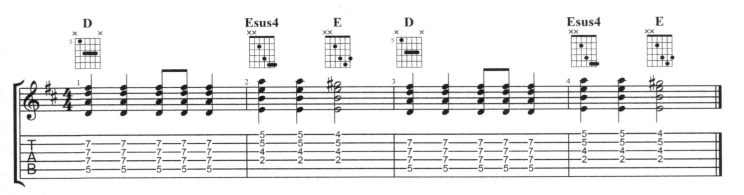

As I mentioned earlier, suspended barre chords are less common on the sixth string, although the sus4 isn't unheard of. To play it, simply finger a major barre chord and flatten your little finger onto the third string.

Note that there are two ways to fret this chord. If you are moving between B Major and Bsus4 it is often easier to flatten the fourth finger as shown in diagram one. But if you have to move to Bsus4 in a hurry you might want to finger the chord in the more classical way shown in diagram two. Don't worry too much if the note on the second string gets muted.

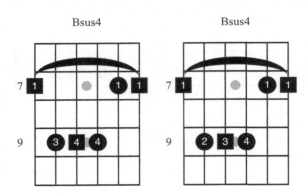

I've demonstrated that movement here with a B Major and Bsus4 chord.

Example 7i:

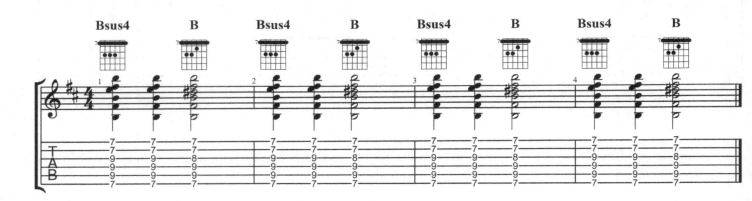

There isn't really a useful/easy standard voicing of a suspended 2nd chord on the sixth string, however this voicing that uses your thumb to play the bass note is not a bad shout. I do stress though that most guitarists would avoid playing a sus2 chord off the sixth string because it's so much easier to play them on the fifth string.

Hook your thumb around the back of the neck and onto the 7th fret of the sixth string. Use the pad to play the note and let your thumb extend over the string to mute the 5th string.

Add your little finger on the 9th fret of the fourth string and then place your first finger on the 6th fret of the third string. Finally, place your second finger on the 7ths fret of the second string.

Strum from the sixth to the second string and listen to ensure the fifth string is muted.

As an additional advantage, your third finger is free to hammer onto the 8th fret of the third string for a beautiful sus2 to major movement. I've shown this in the example below.

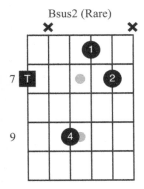

This example uses the chord above and a hammer on to move from the sus2 to the major voicing. .

Example 7j:

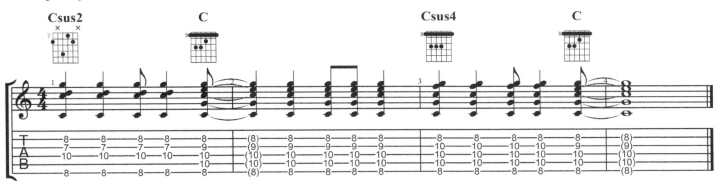

Example 7k gets creative with a sus4 chord.

Example 7k:

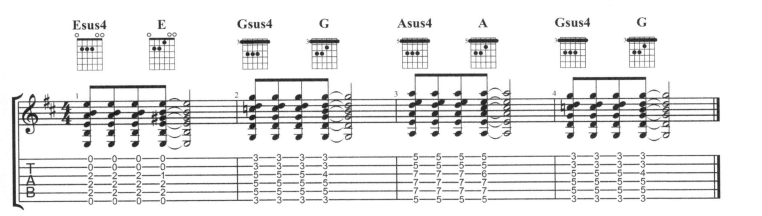

Overall, you'll probably find that the suspended barre chords on the fifth string are the most accessible to play at first, so spend most of your time focusing on those.

In the next few chapters, things will get a little jazzier as we explore Major 7th and Minor 7th chords.

Chapter Eight: Major 7th Chords

Major 7th and Minor 7th chords (along with dominant 7 chords), form the backbone of jazz music from about 1930 onwards. However, you will still find them occasionally turning up in pop songs to create a richer, deeper harmony than a simple major or minor triad.

As with dominant 7 chords, Major 7th chords are a four-note chord created by adding a major 3rd on top of a major chord.

C Major is formed from the notes C, E, G.

C Major 7th is formed from the notes C, E, G, B.

Normally musicians use the shorthand "Maj7" to write Major 7ths, however you will often see them written as $\triangle$7 too. For example, C$\triangle$7.

The most useful Maj7 barre chord shape on the sixth string doesn't technically require you to barre your finger, but as it contains no open strings you can still move it anywhere on the neck as normal.

Here's the chord diagram for CMaj7. Use your first finger to play the note on the sixth string and your second to play the note on the second string. Your third and fourth fingers should fall nicely into place on fourth and third strings.

Notice the X on the fifth and first strings, which means they shouldn't sound. To mute the fifth string, allow your first finger to go slightly flat to touch it and stop it sounding.

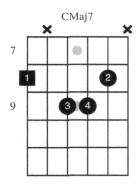

Strum the chord one string at a time and make sure the fifth string is muted. Don't strum the first string.

Once you can play the chord cleanly, play the following example that teaches you to move the chord to different locations on the sixth string. Remove and replace your hand each time – don't cheat and slide the chord along the strings. You need to build some muscle memory!

Example 8a:

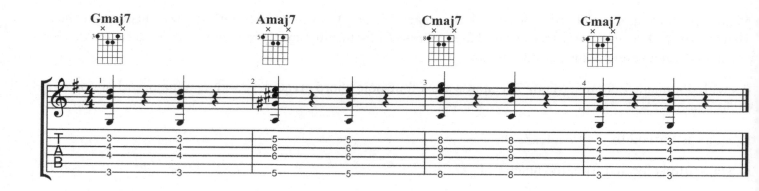

The Maj7 voicing with a root on the fifth string is more of a traditional barre chord. Play the following DMaj7 at the 5th fret on the fifth string.

Form the chord by placing your first finger before adding your third, second, then fourth.

Strumming the highest string is optional and gives you a subtly different timbre. Also, if you don't want to play the highest string, then there's no need to actually barre across the strings, which makes the voicing a lot easier.

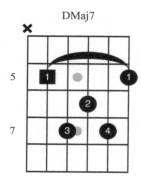

Try playing the chord at different points along the fifth string before studying this exercise that teaches you to move between Maj7 chords on the fifth and sixth strings.

Example 8b:

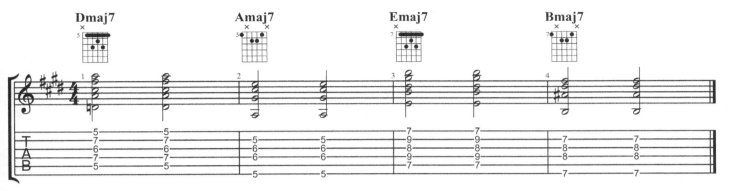

The following exercise is similar but adds in a few open chords.

Example 8c:

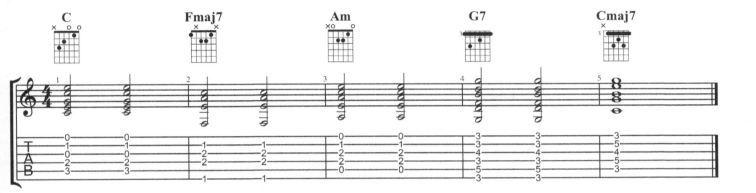

Finally, here's a GMaj7 barre chord voicing on the fourth string. Place your first finger on the fourth string, then barre across the top three strings with the side of your third finger.

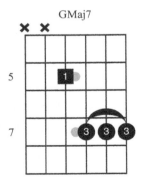

Again, practice placing and removing this chord at different points along the neck before working through the next few exercises that move between Maj7th chords.

Example 8d moves between Maj7 chords on all three strings.

Example 8d:

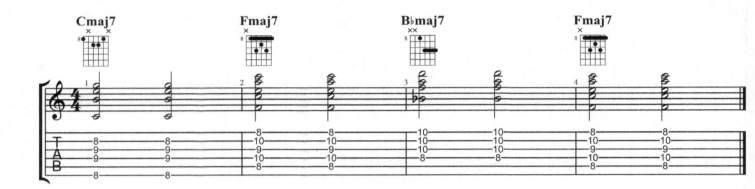

This idea reintroduces dominant 7 chords and combines them with Maj7 chords on all three string sets.

Example 8e:

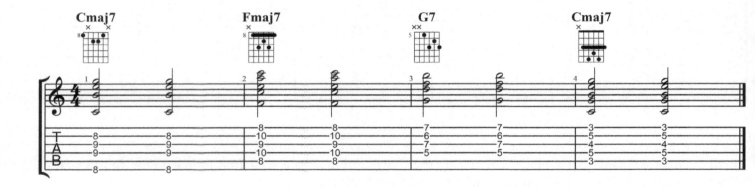

Finally, here's an example that moves between open strings and barre chord voicings of Major, Minor, 7, and Maj7 chords.

Example 8f:

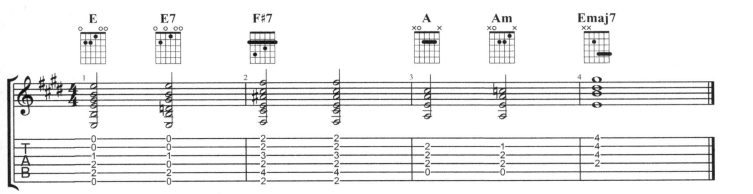

We will cover more chord progressions after we have studied Minor 7 chords in the next chapter. For now, make sure you can move smoothly between Maj7 chords before you move on.

Chapter Nine: Minor 7th Chords

Minor 7 chords are probably more common in pop, funk, soul and jazz than Maj7 chords, as they have a relaxed, yet rich colour.

They are a four-note chord created by adding a minor 3rd on top of a minor chord.

C Minor 7 is formed from the notes C, Eb, G.

C Minor 7th is formed from the notes C, Eb, G, Bb.

Normally musicians use the shorthand m7 to write Minor 7ths, however you will occasionally see them written as -7 too. For example, C-7. This is quite an old way to notate them and is not so common anymore.

The most useful m7 barre chord shape on the sixth string doesn't technically require you to barre your finger, but as it contains no open strings you can still move it anywhere on the neck.

There are a couple of common ways to play m7 barre chords on the sixth string. The first is to use one finger for each note.

Here's the chord diagram for Cm7. Use your first finger to play the note on the sixth string and your fourth to play the note on the second string. Your second and third fingers should fall nicely into place on the fourth and third strings.

As with CMaj7, there is an X on the fifth and first strings, which means they shouldn't sound. To mute the fifth string, allow your first finger to go slightly flat to touch it and stop it sounding.

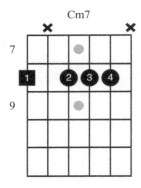

Strum the chord one string at a time and make sure the fifth string is muted. Don't strum the first string.

The other way to fret the chord seems a little strange at first, but it's actually quite common because it leaves your first and fourth fingers free to play other notes.

The idea is to play the bass string with your *second* finger, then use your third finger to barre across the top three or four strings. It's definitely a different approach but a popular one because it offers a lot of melodic possibilities.

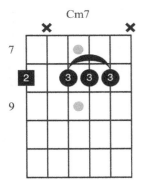

Cm7

Try both voicings and see which you prefer. Just learn one for now and stick with it throughout this chapter. You can always come back to explore the other voicing later.

Once you can play the Cm7 cleanly, play the following example that teaches you to move it to different locations on the sixth string.

Example 9a:

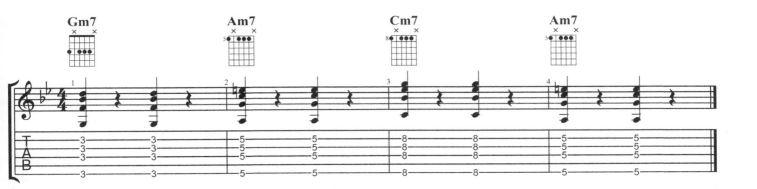

This example moves between Maj7, 7, and m7 chords, all on the sixth string.

Example 9b:

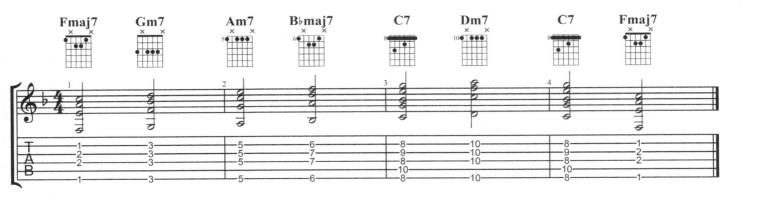

The m7 voicing on the fifth string should be one of the easier shapes for you to learn now. It's very similar to the minor barre chord you learned in Chapter Two. The only thing to watch out for is the placement of the third and second fingers. Make sure they are on their tips, so the all-important note on the third string rings clearly. It's easy to accidentally mute this string and it's the most important character note of the chord.

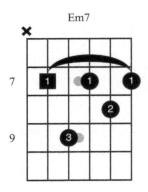

As before, remove and replace this chord at different points along the string to build your muscle memory.

When you have gained some confidence, play through this example that contains Maj7, 7, and m7 chords, all on the fifth string.

Example 9c:

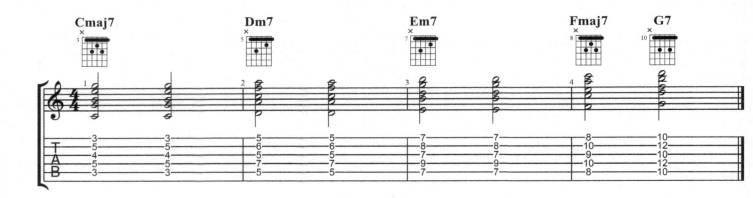

Here's the fourth string voicing of the m7 chord. There's no traditional barre here, but as there are no open strings you can move the chord anywhere you like along the string.

This fingering might seem awkward at first, but if you place your first finger on the fourth string before adding your second and third fingers together, then finally add the little finger on the third string, you'll find it easier.

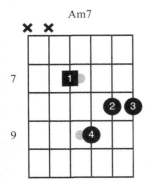

As before, place and remove the chord at different points along the string before tackling this example that contains Maj7, 7, and m7 chords, all on the fourth string.

Example 9d:

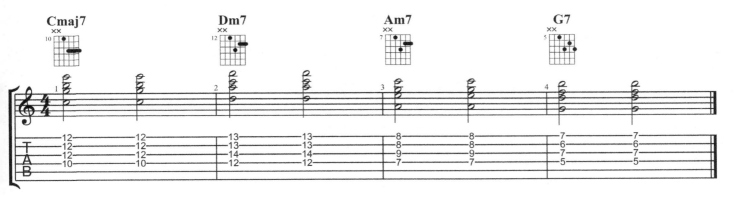

In the next example, you're going to play just m7 voicings across all three string groups.

Example 9e:

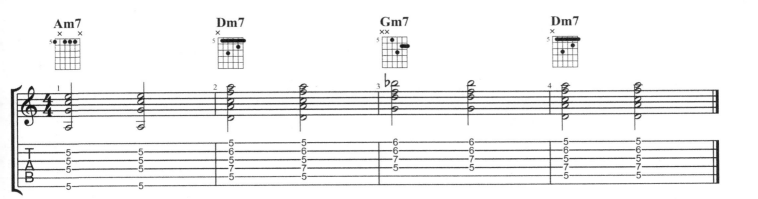

This example is a little longer and combines different Maj7, 7 and m7 chords across all three string groups.

Example 9f:

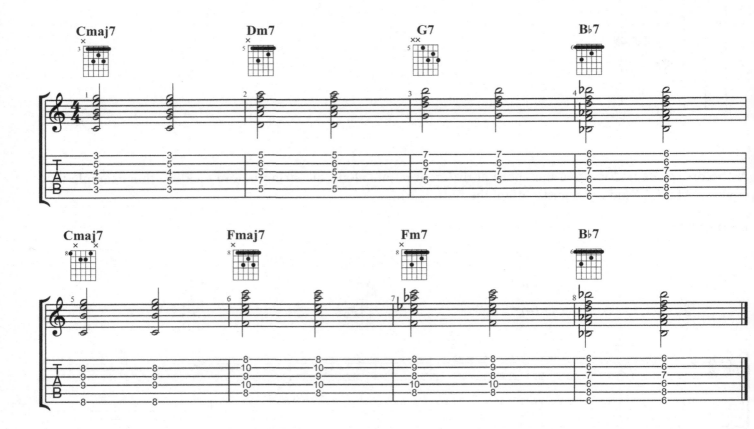

Finally, here's an example that introduces a few open chords into the mix.

Example 9g:

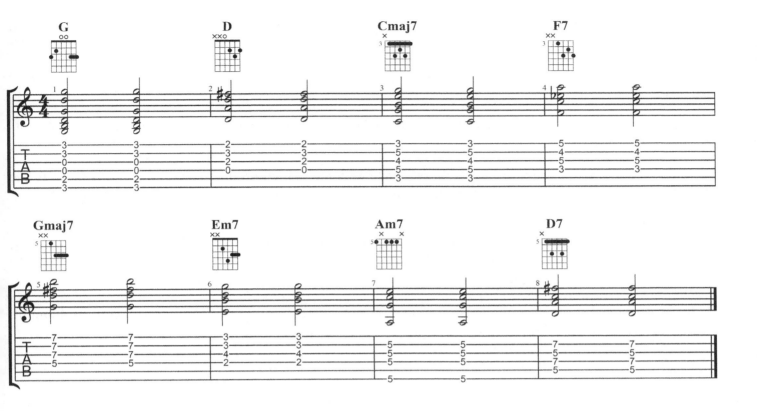

Congratulations! You've now learnt the most common barre chords you'll need to be able to play through almost any piece of music. Under your fingers you have barre chord voicings for Major, Minor, 7, Sus2 and 4, Maj7, 7, and m7 chords.

Of course, there are some chords that are less common but it's important not to take too much on board at once when you're learning.

Now all these chords are under your fingers, move on to the next chapter where I've written some practice sequences for you to work through.

Chapter Ten: Practice Progressions

The chord sequences in this chapter are here to help you memorize more fully the chords you've covered in the book.

Each one is written out as chord symbols, but with no notation… just like a chord chart you might come across in a "fake" book.

Each one can be played in an almost unlimited number of ways by choosing to play barre chords with roots on different strings.

For example, you might begin by playing a sequence with the first chord on the sixth string and move to the closest voicing of the next chord on the fifth string. However, the next time through you might play the first chord with a root on the fifth or fourth string and move to a new voicing for the next chord, etc.

Every chord change offers you at least three different options of barre chord location, and by beginning in different places on the neck, you'll naturally push your chord voicings into different territories and quickly learn where all the chords lie on the neck.

Begin by looking for the closest voicing on an adjacent string, but don't be afraid to explore by jumping around, or even playing all the chords with root notes on the same string.

Example 10a:

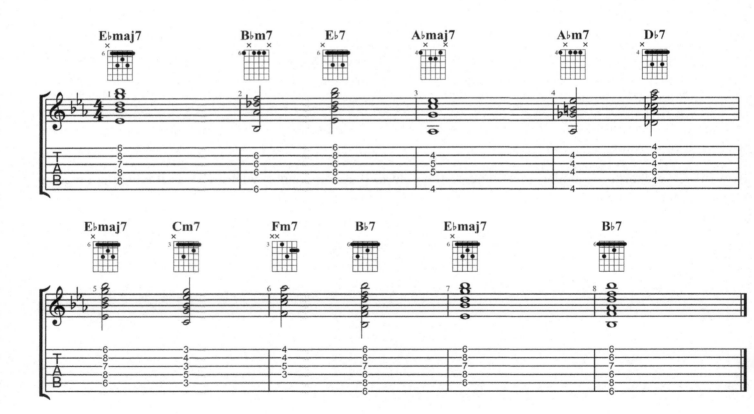

Example 10b:

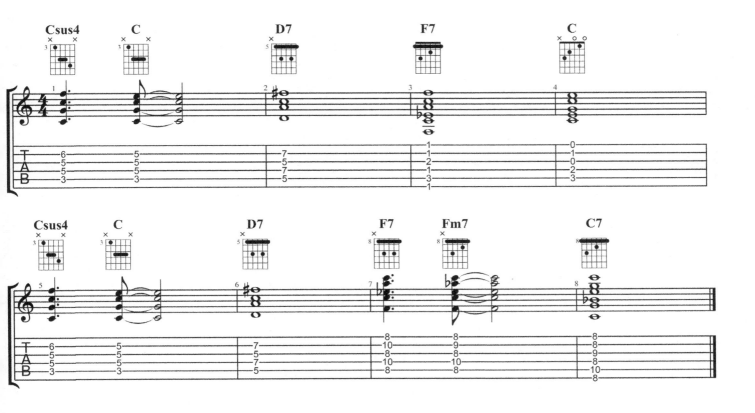

Example 10c:

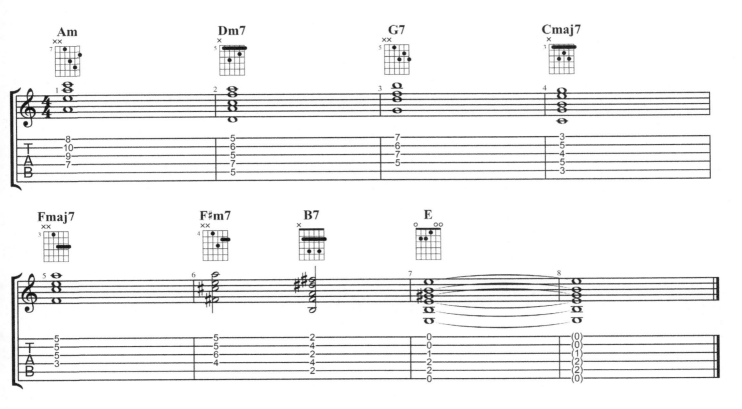

Example 10d:

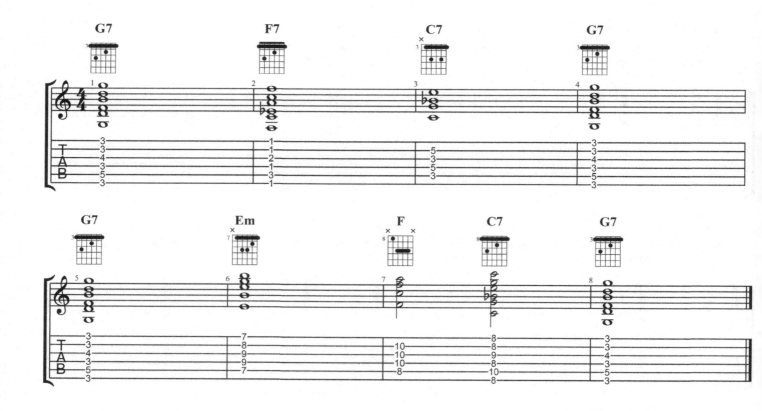

Example 10e:

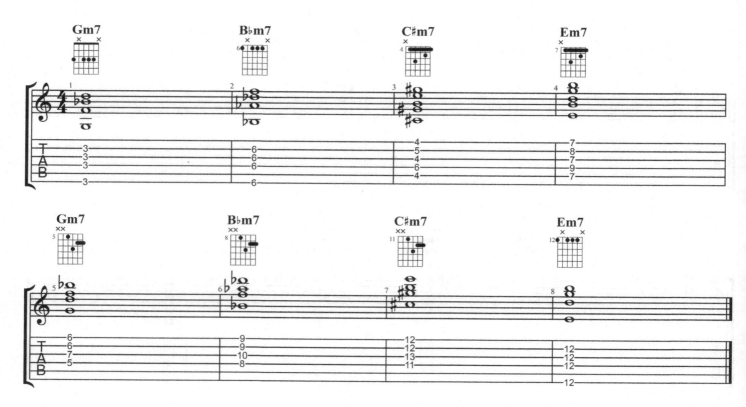

Example 10f:

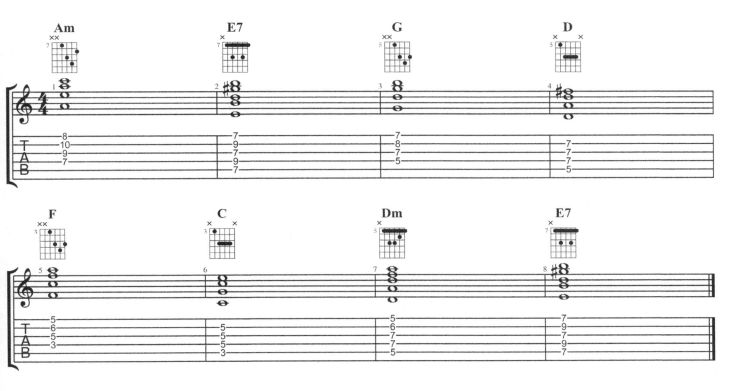

Example 10g:

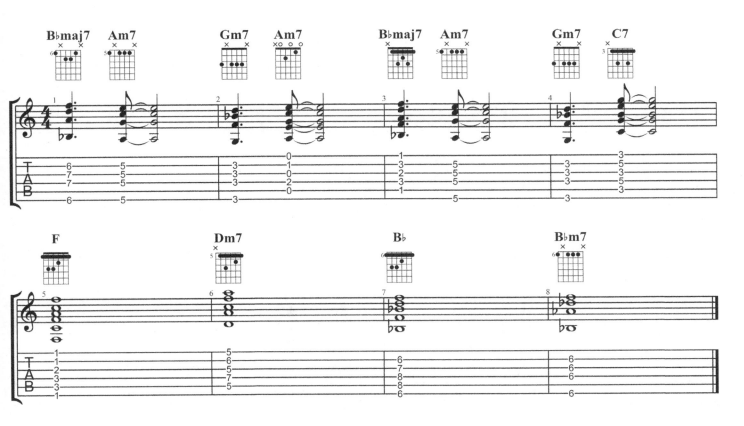

Example 10h:

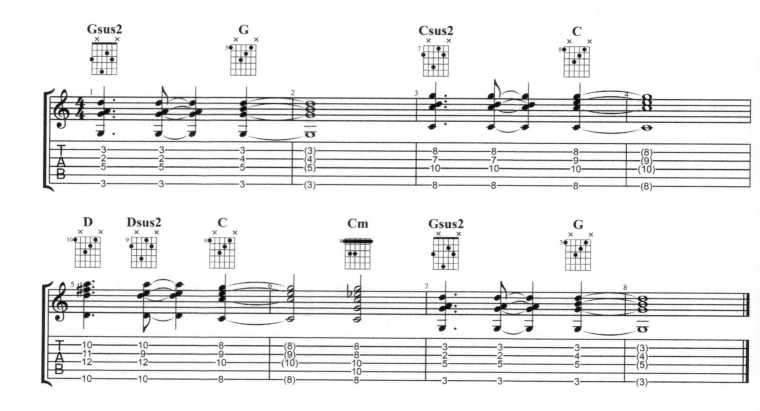

Example 10i:

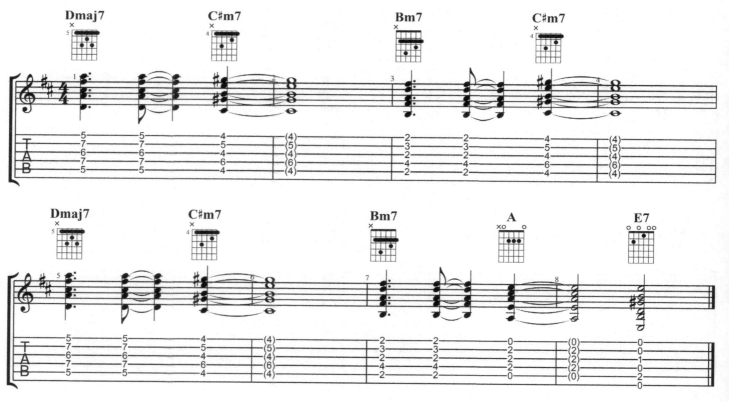

Example 10j:

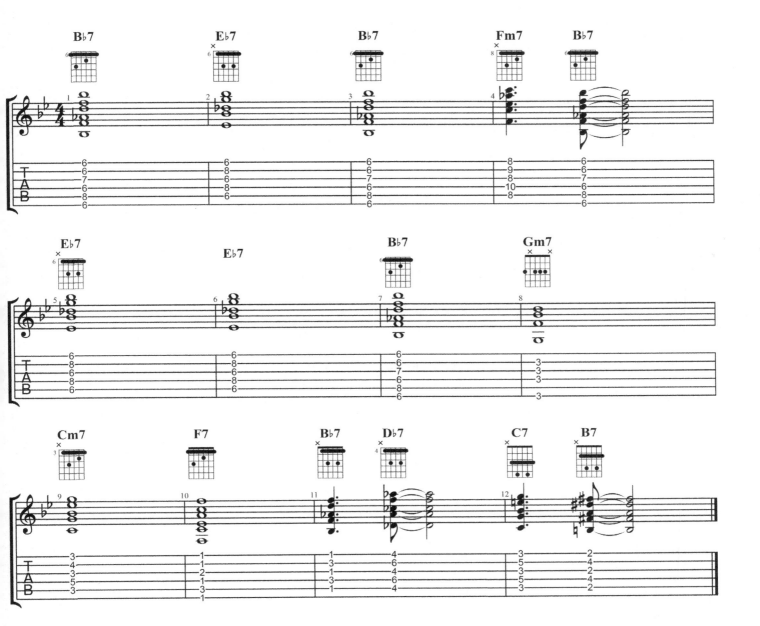

Chapter Eleven: m7b5, mMaj7 chords and Chord Chains

I don't want this to become a theory book, but I wanted to quickly show you some interesting chord sequences that will help you to understand the construction of Major, Minor, Maj7, 7 and m7 chords.

Hopefully, you'll remember that Major and Minor chords contain three notes, and to create any type of 7th chord we have to add an additional note.

For example, the chord formulas for the above chord types with a root note of C are shown in the table below:

Chord	Formula	Notes
C Major	1 3 5	C E G
C Major 7	1 3 5 7	C E G B
C7	1 3 5 b7	C E G Bb
C Minor	1 b3 5	C Eb G
C Minor 7	1 b3 5 b7	C Eb G Bb

Now, if you also remember that Major and Minor barre chords double some notes in the chord voicings, you'll quickly start to understand a bit about how these chords are constructed and formed on the guitar.

For example, here is a fifth string barre chord of C Major. Notice that the note C is doubled on the fifth and third strings.

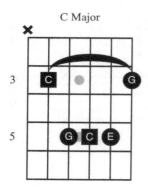

Now look back at the table. To create a CMaj7 chord from a C Major chord, I need to add the note B. The note B is a half-step (semitone) below the note C, so I simply lower the C note on the 3rd string by one fret to B.

Doing this creates the CMaj7 you learned in Chapter Eight.

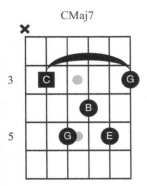

CMaj7

Look at the table again. To create a C7 chord I need to remove the note B from the CMaj7 chord and add the note Bb. The note Bb is one half-step below B, so I simply lower it by one fret to Bb.

Doing this creates the C7 you learned in Chapter Two.

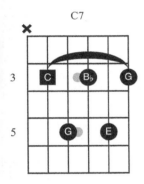

C7

Play these three chords in sequence and watch how the note on the third string is lowered by a half-step each time.

It's also the intro to the song *Kiss Me*, by Sixpence None the Richer!

Example 11a:

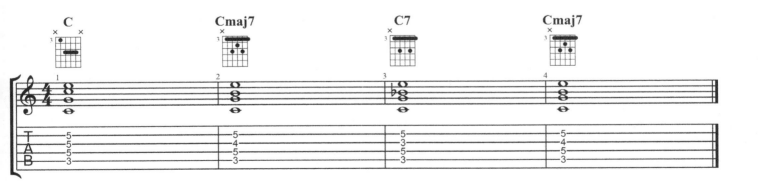

Now try the same process with a C Minor chord.

To create a Cm7 chord from a C Minor we simply need to add a Bb, which is found a whole step below the root on the third string.

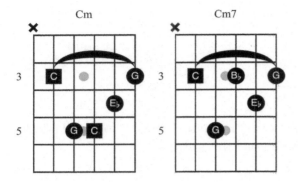

Try playing both these chords.

Example 11b:

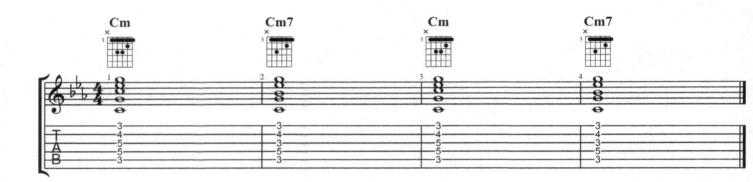

There's another relationship you should be aware of too. Dominant 7 chords and Minor 7 chords sound very different, yet only have one note different between them. Look at the table above and you'll see that a C7 contains the notes C, E, G, and Bb, and Cm7 contains the notes C, Eb, G, and Bb.

This time, we will transition all the way from C Major to Cm7 by only moving one note at a time.

Example 11c:

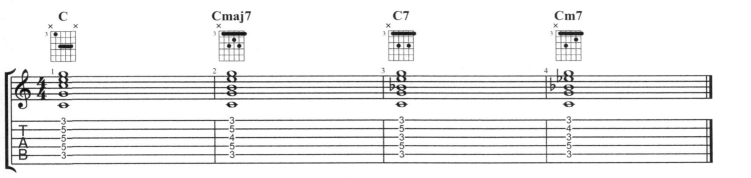

When you begin to look at chord relationships like this, you really start to understand a lot about how chords are constructed.

Here's the same sequence played with a root on the sixth string.

Example 11d:

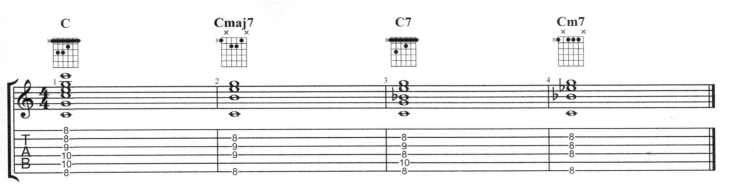

And here it is with a root on the fourth string.

Example 11e:

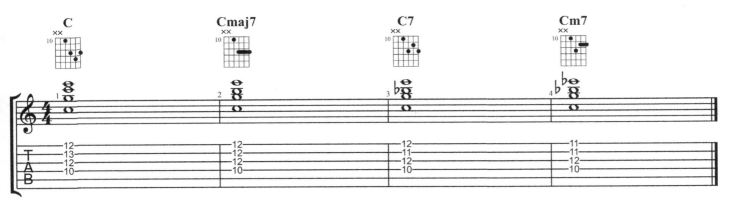

Memorize the following rules:

- A Major 7th note is always a half-step below the root

- A Dominant 7 or Minor 7th note is always a whole step below the root

Also,

- Major chords can be extended to create Maj7 chords and dominant 7 chords

- Minor chords can be extended to create m7 chords

After working through this chapter, you might be asking, "What happens if you add a *major 7th* to a minor chord?"

Well, the answer is that you create a chord called a *Minor/Major 7th* (written CmMaj7). It's got a very specific sound and you'll often hear it used in movie soundtracks. Here are the three most common barre chord voicings of CmMaj7.

Watch out for the muted fifth and first strings in the first diagram. I play this chord with four fingers, but if you're clever you can barre with your first finger and adjust it slightly to mute the fifth string.

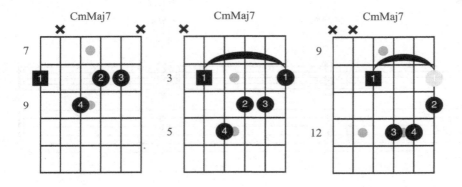

Example 11f:

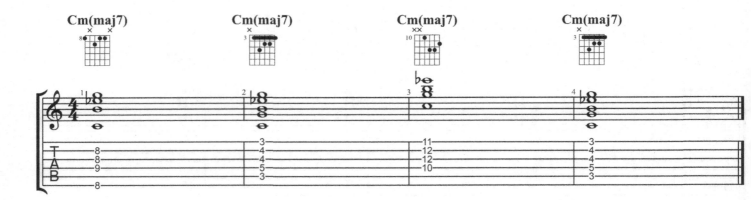

96

You might also be thinking "Can we play with any other notes of the chord?" The answer is yes!

A common jazz chord you'll see is called a "minor 7 flat 5" (written m7b5) As you might be able to guess, it is formed by taking a m7 chord and flattening the 5th note. So, instead of the Cm7 notes of C, Eb, G, Bb, the notes in Cm7b5 are C, Eb, *Gb,* Bb.

These chords crop up all the time in jazz, so you need to know them if you're heading in a jazzy direction.

Here are the three most common barre chord voicings of the m7b5 chord.

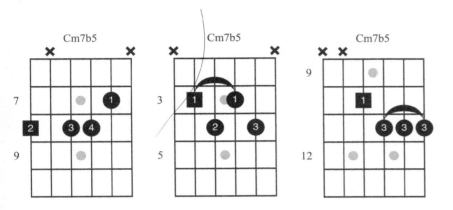

Example 11g:

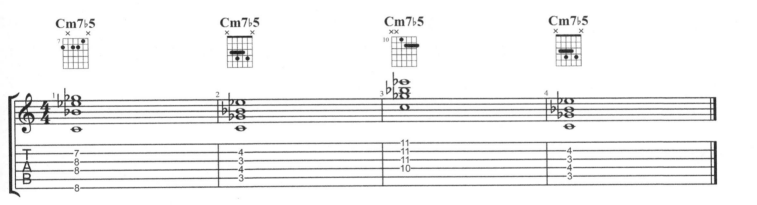

Spend some time learning the m7b5 and mMaj7 barre chord voicings as you did in previous chapters.

Now let's add these two chord types to the table we started earlier. I've arranged it so that only one note changes between each chord as you move down the table. Try playing through the sequence with barre chords on each string group.

Chord	Formula	Notes
Cm7b5	1 b3 b5 b7	C Eb Gb Bb
Cm7	1 b3 5 b7	C Eb G Bb
C7	1 3 5 b7	C E G Bb
CMaj7	1 3 5 7	C E G B
C Major	1 3 5	C E G
C Minor	1 b3 5	C Eb G
CmMaj7	1 b3 5 7	C Eb G B

While you can definitely consider this table "extracurricular", it's very useful to know how to *construct* any chord you need and understand the differences and relationships between all the chord types.

Finally, here are some chord sequences that introduce these new chord voicings and combine them with the barre chords you already know. As always, play through each sequence in multiple ways, beginning on different strings and moving to different locations for subsequent chords.

Example 11h:

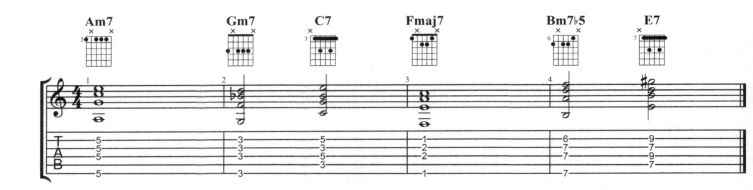

Example 11i:

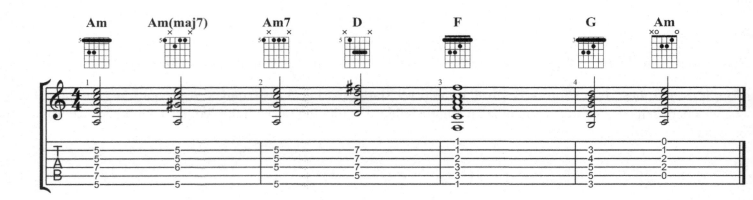

98

Example 11j:

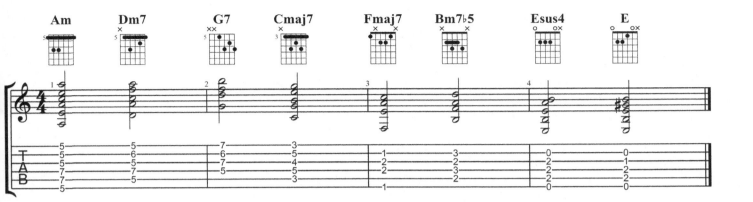

Conclusion

I hope you've enjoyed this guide to learning and playing barre chords. I've tried to cover all of the basics and give you everything you need to tackle any song you'll want to learn as an improving beginner.

I'll leave you with a piece of advice given to me by my teacher, Neil, when I started to sightread difficult jazz tunes and began to come across complex chords I didn't know how to play.

He said, "In an emergency, just play the letters!"

This became a lifesaver for me on more than one occasion.

What it means is that if you can recognise the *type* of chord in front of you, but you don't know how to play any complex written version of it, simplify it down to the basic chord type.

For example:

If you're playing in a band don't know how to play an unexpected chord... maybe something like C7#11, C7b9, or C7b9#5 etc, just play C7.

If you don't know how to play CMaj7#11, you could just play CMaj7 or C Major.

If you don't know how to play Cm9b5, you can play Cm7b5.

OK, you might play a slight dissonance for a second, but most people won't notice, and you'll get through the tune. But make sure you learn the correct chord next time you're in the practice room!

Some less common chords you may encounter are included in the appendix below, so you'll have a reference if you come across something that's not been covered in the book.

Have fun!

Joseph

Appendix

This brief appendix covers some less common barre chord voicings that you might come across in your musical journey.

Let's begin with *diminished* chords. Their formula is 1 b3 b5 (C Eb Gb). You may wish to play the rootless version of the fourth string barre, as playing the lowest note with the first finger creates a challenging stretch.

Note that you can also play an easier-to-fret Diminished 7th instead of a Diminished chord, so see below if you find these voicings challenging.

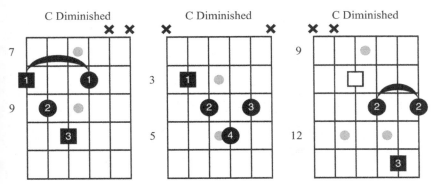

Example 12a:

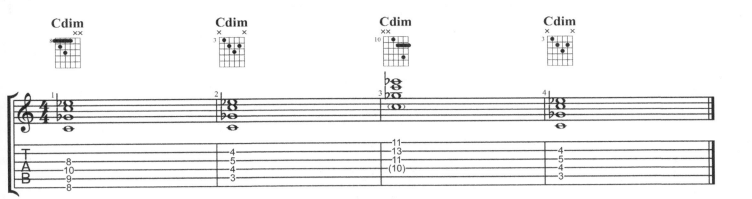

These are *diminished 7th* (Dim7) chords. Their formula is 1 b3 b5 bb7 (C Eb Gb A).

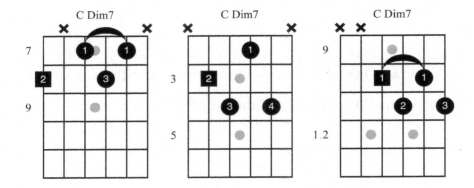

Example 12b:

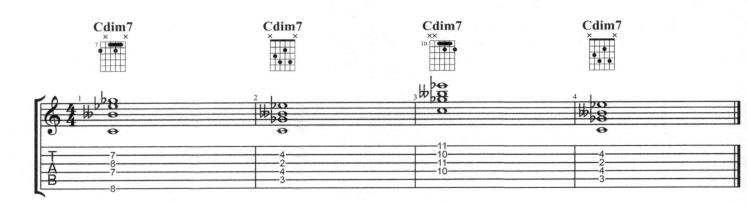

The next set of chords are called *augmented*. Their formula is 1 3 #5 (C E G#).

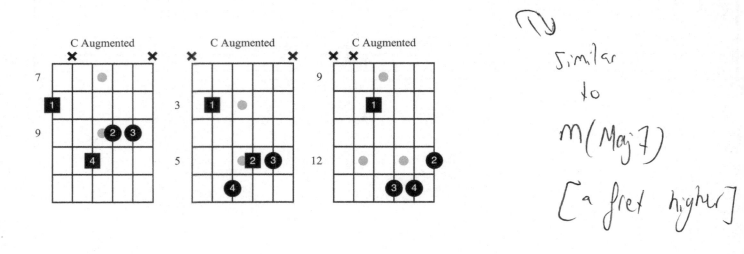

Similar
to
m(Maj7)
[a fret higher]

Example 12c:

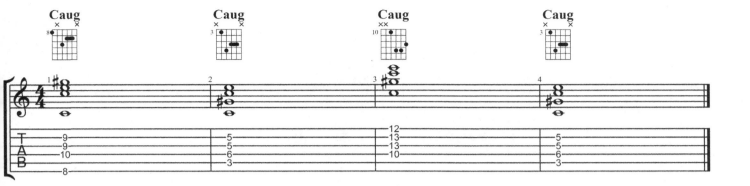

And these are *augmented 7ths* (or "7#5"). Their formula is 1 3 #5 b7 (C E G# Bb).

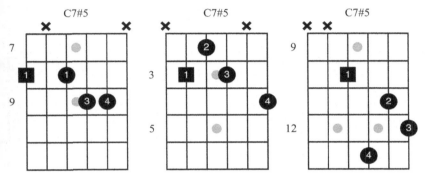

Example 12d:

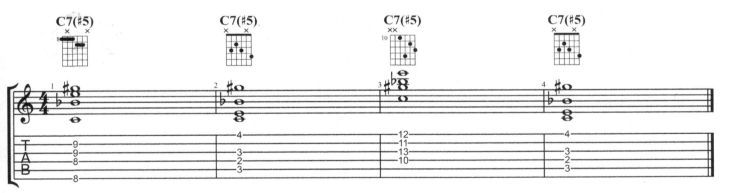

Next are Major 6 chords. These aren't too uncommon. Their formula is 1 3 5 6 (C E G A).

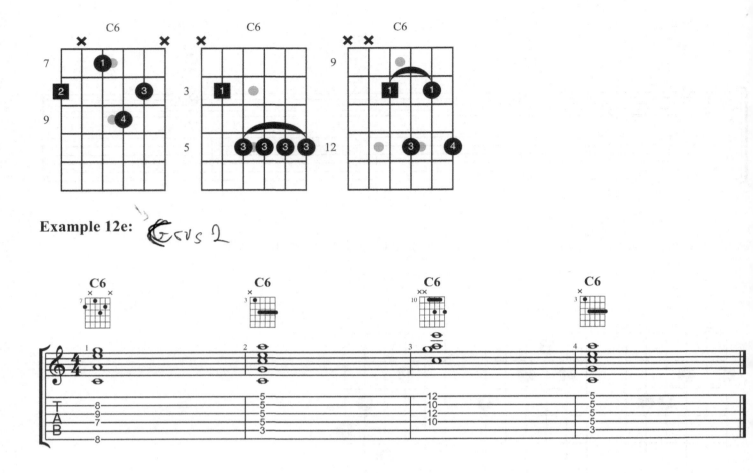

Example 12e: ⎧ *I C V S 2*

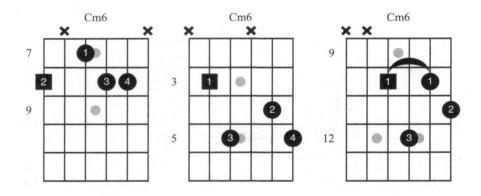

And here are the set of minor 6 chords which you'll also see occasionally. Their formula is 1 b3 5 6 (C E G A).

Example 12f:

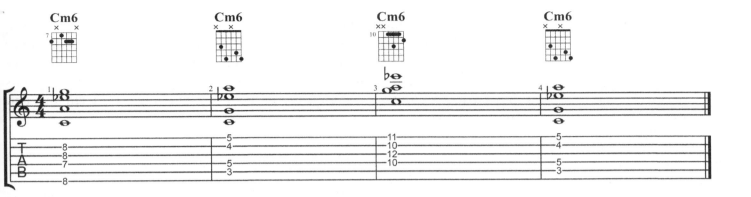

I could fill this book with various different permutations of *altered dominant* chords (7b9, 7#9, 7#9b5, etc.), of the kind you might find in a jazz tune, but really those chords deserve their own book. If you're interested in exploring jazz chords then might I humbly suggest my book *The First 100 Jazz Chords for Guitar*, before moving on to *Jazz Guitar Chord Mastery*.

Either way, the chords I've given you in this appendix should cover many of the less common situations you come across in your journey as a musician.

Have fun playing through them and discovering new sounds that you can also use in your song writing.

Bestselling Guitar Books for Beginners from Joseph Alexander

The First 100 Chords for Guitar is not simply a list of chords, it's a complete guitar method for beginners that teaches you how to practice for a lifetime of good guitar habits. From the most basic chords, right through to some rich and exciting advanced voicings, you will be guided in small friendly steps. Throughout, there is an emphasis on using the correct fingers, changing chords smoothly, building great technique and developing creativity.

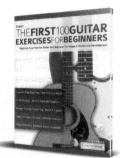

Learn beginner guitar skills that will last a lifetime. As well as teaching you the basic skills of guitar playing, such as how to fret and pick chords, from the outset you'll be taught skills that will set you up for a lifetime of enjoyment with the guitar. Unlock countless pieces of guitar music with **The First 100 Guitar Exercises for Beginners**.

The First 100 Strumming Patterns for Guitar draws on years of distilled teaching experience to bring you a detailed, step-by-step guide to rhythm and strumming – from ground zero to rhythm hero. The music you learn here will form the backbone of any music you play and allow you to play pretty much anything you encounter on your musical journey.

Quickly master the guitar and build good habits for life-long learning. **Beginner's Guitar Lessons: The Essential Guide**, teaches you to play the right way from the first time you pick up the instrument. Learn to hold and strum the guitar, play in time, change chords, finger pick, plus much more. There are many common mistakes that beginner guitarists make that limit their musical development. This book forms a foundation of good technique and skills that will last a lifetime.

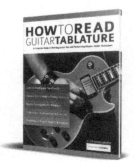

How to Read Guitar Tablature is the ideal music stand companion and gig bag essential. Never be confused again by the odd signs and abbreviations that appear in tab, and expand your technique repertoire as you learn! Rather than a cold glossary of terms, it contains tips, insights and more than 90 recorded musical examplesthat demonstrate the techniques themselves.

Made in the USA
Las Vegas, NV
12 October 2022

57104036R00059